*from the folks at
Xmas, 1978*

ARE YOU ALWAYS "BUSY" YET NEVER SEEM TO GET ANYTHING DONE?

Alan Lakein has written this practical, no-nonsense guide to managing your personal and business time. He shows you how to set short-term and long-term goals, establish priorities, organize a daily schedule, and achieve better self-understanding. He even provides tips for building willpower, creating quiet time, defeating unpleasant tasks, and keeping yourself on target. IBM, The Bank of America, Gloria Steinem, and thousands of business people, professionals, homemakers, and students have benefited from his program—now you can make it work for you.

Time is life. This book is your key to liberating all the vital energies and vast potential you possess.

HOW TO
GET CONTROL
OF YOUR TIME
AND YOUR LIFE

by *Alan Lakein*

A SIGNET BOOK
NEW AMERICAN LIBRARY
TIMES MIRROR

SIGNET TRADEMARK REG. U.S. PAT. OFF. AND FOREIGN COUNTRIES
REGISTERED TRADEMARK—MARCA REGISTRADA
HECHO EN CHICAGO, U.S.A.

SIGNET, SIGNET CLASSICS, MENTOR, PLUME AND MERIDIAN BOOKS
are published by The New American Library, Inc.,
1301 Avenue of the Americas, New York, New York 10019

FIRST SIGNET PRINTING, JUNE, 1974

11 12 13 14 15 16 17

PRINTED IN THE UNITED STATES OF AMERICA

To Jeanne

Contents

1. WHY YOU SHOULD CARE ABOUT YOUR TIME

TIME IS LIFE. It is irreversible and irreplaceable. To waste your time is to waste your life, but to master your time is to master your life and make the most of it.

As a Time Planning and Life Goals Consultant, I have created a new system which is helping thousands of people right now to determine the best use of their time—and so gain control of their lives.

I'm not a "time and motion" organizer, trying to get everything done in the shortest time with the fewest wasted motions. That kind of efficiency means taking the thinking out of an activity and reducing it to a series of mechanical routines. There is no attempt to keep it fun or interesting, so you might even say that such extreme clockwatching takes the life right out of an activity, along with the thought.

I try to put more thinking into what people do, not take the thinking out. If you follow my suggestions, you'll probably find yourself thinking more about how you really want to use your time, working less hard, doing more of the things you've always wanted to do, and enjoying your life a lot more.

So please don't call me an efficiency expert. I'm an "effectiveness expert." Effectiveness means selecting the best task to do from all the possibilities available and then doing it the best way. Making the right choices about how you'll use your time is more important than doing efficiently whatever job happens to be around. Efficiency is fine in its place, but to my mind effectiveness is a much more important goal.

Some of the techniques of my system may surprise you. For instance, suppose you've got ten minutes before you must go to the dentist. If you're like most people, you'll fritter that time away. But I can show you how to invest those ten minutes so you can make a solid start on any big job you may have been putting off—like redecorating your home or analyzing your production costs. At the same time, I will help you to eliminate procrastination and maintain the momentum you need to get the job done.

In this book you'll learn about the experiences of my clients, my family and myself in applying my techniques. And you'll see that my system is not inflexible, mechanical or burdensome. Far from it! It's fun to learn and fun to experiment with. The benefits come immediately, and then continue to grow.

My system for effective time use has worked successfully for such corporate clients as A.T. & T., Bank of America, I.B.M., Lever Brothers, and Standard Oil Company of California; for numerous local and federal agencies; for such busy people as recording star Neil Diamond; feminist and writer Gloria Steinem; designer Milton Glaser; Mike McCloskey, Executive Director of the Sierra Club; William Ball, General Director of the American Conservatory Theatre; Mike Murphy, Esalen Institute president; Michael Butler, producer of "Hair;" and for thousands of executives, professionals, entrepreneurs, homemakers, students, and others who consult me during my seminars or on an individual basis.

I feel strongly about the value of my system because it has given me control of my own life. The system can also work successfully for *your* life and what *you* want to get out of it. I'm not necessarily trying to show you how to become president of your company or how to juggle simultaneous careers as office worker and mother. With my system, you *can* achieve such goals—if they really are your goals. But you can also become a more effective college student, chess player, candlemaker or international playboy. It's entirely up to you.

And please remember: There is no such thing as lack of time. We all have plenty of time to do everything we really want to do. If, like so many people, you're "too busy" to get things done, keep in mind that there are plenty of people who are even busier than you are who manage to get more done than you do. They don't have more time than you have. They just use their time to better advantage! Effective time use—like driving a car—is a skill that can be acquired, and in this book I have assembled all the tools you'll need. I'll show you sensible, practical ways so you can be the master of the clock—not its slave—and do what you want with your life.

When all is said and done, there simply is nothing more important in your life than your time. I can't give you any more time than you already have. We all must live on 168 hours a week. But I can help you to use the time you have more effectively.

So let's begin!

2. YOUR PAYOFF: CONTROL OF YOUR LIFE

Control IS A KEY concept in this book. Since no synonym can do justice to everything that I mean by *control,* let me illustrate.

Make your hand into a fist. Squeeze your hand as hard as you can and feel the tension. If you hold the fist tight for even a few minutes, your hand will ache with the effort. Such a tensed, strained fist has few (peaceful) uses.

Next, drop your hand to your side. Keep all your muscles as loose as possible. You can't get much productive work out of your hand in that position, either.

Now raise your hand slowly in front of you and make it come alive. Gradually move the fingers and feel the muscles respond with good tone and control. Here is a hand that can get something done!

The kind of control I am recommending is in many ways analogous to good muscle tone. It is the sort of control over your time (and your life) that is neither too tight (i.e., compulsive, restrained, obsessive) nor too loose (i.e., apathetic, indifferent, lazy). This kind of control will help you get things done and also allows you to be flexible and spontaneous.

The ideal is balance.

Beware the Time Nut

The purpose of this book is emphatically not to turn you into a compulsive clockwatcher, or into someone who is constantly busy or aggressively efficient. To be more specific, here are three notorious characters that neither I nor anybody else enjoys having around:

The *overorganized person* is always making lists, updating lists, losing lists. When asked to do something, he tends to

14

spend much time considering every possibility, planning every detail, making sure that he has every base covered. He doesn't move without first planning the smallest detail, and consequently he often doesn't even get around to doing many things he should. He is more interested in feeling organized in his head than in accomplishing anything. If he doesn't get around to doing what he planned today—well, he'll just make a better plan tomorrow. He's so intent on being well-organized that he's often blind to changes, new opportunities, and the needs of others.

The *overdoer* is so busy doing things that he has no time to assess their true value. He is a hard person to approach, even with a time-saving idea. He's generally disliked because he tells everyone else what to do. He lacks spontaneity and flexibility. He's terribly efficient, but as often as not is eagerly clambering up the wrong tree. With every minute of his time, both at home and at work, filled with activity, he never has a moment to relax.

The *time nut* is overwhelmingly preoccupied with time. He makes himself and everyone else nervous with his concern about never wasting a minute. He's always rushing around to meet an impossible schedule. If a meeting starts even a minute late, he frets and fumes. He keeps careful records in great detail of what he does every day. He knows how to save eleven seconds eating his cereal! Not an easy person to work or live with.

If you think that trying to "get control" of your time and your life means becoming super-organized, super-busy, or preoccupied with every moment as it slips by, let me assure you that this is not the case. Each of the three types sketched above has taken a potentially valuable trait and turned it into a liability. Each is as badly off as the person who's totally disorganized, never does what he says he is going to do, never plans ahead, or goes through life from one crisis to another.

Neither extreme is desirable. Too much organization is as ineffective as too little. But there is no right answer. Different people require varying degrees of structure and spontaneity in their lives. What's more, the same person has different needs at different ages, at different times of the year, in different situations. The person who is well-organized at work may be very haphazard about his non-work activities. The person who at thirty has a clear set of goals and knows exactly how he wants to use his time and his life may find that at forty he must break free of such plans if he is to grow.

You're the Judge

No part of my system is intended to be used inflexibly, automatically or mechanically. Its sole purpose and justification is to help set you free from internal and external restraints, *not* to take away one iota of your freedom and individuality.

Time use is a highly personal, individual matter of choice, and you must be the final judge of how to apply the suggestions presented in this book. It's important that you compare all of the things I say with the way you function best. As you read, assess your own strengths and weaknesses. Consider your own time problems and set priorities for what to improve. Don't be afraid to mark up the book, reading with pen or pencil to make the book yours. Underline the key ideas, and makes notes in the margins. List the numbers of the pages that are most important to you in the inside front cover for easy reference.

Pick and choose among the ideas. Recognize that different techniques work for different people, and that there are times when good advice for one person is useless for another. Select the ideas that will benefit you the most, and use them to help you lead a more enjoyable and satisfying life.

It doesn't matter whether you're doing office work, housework, school assignments, or just loafing—I'll show you how to do whatever you're doing more effectively. I'll help you separate those tasks that matter from those that don't. Believe me: You can get the important ones done, even if they seem overwhelming, unpleasant, or impossible.

Are you sick and tired of never getting anything done because you never get anything started? I'll show you how to end procrastination once and for all.

Do you want to improve your concentration, brush off distractions and develop stick-to-itiveness? I'll show you how. Do you want to deal with the people around you more effectively? I'll show you how to do that too—and keep them happy besides.

This book offers tested techniques for performing under

pressure, and will show you all the ins and outs of executing a project with tact, precision, and timeliness.

If you're so inclined, this book can help you increase your earning power. Making better use of your time will endear you to your boss, or, if you're in business for yourself, will give you more time to ply your trade.

Above all, this book will show you how to work smarter, not harder, with the end result that you have more time for yourself, your family, and your friends, or time to undertake that dream you've been putting off because you "haven't had the time." You'll feel less at the mercy of the uncontrollable elements of your situation and environment. You'll be better able to improvise, amend, and rearrange such elements to suit your personality, goals, and outlook.

It might sound like a contradiction in terms, but I think that by the end of this book you'll agree with me that the biggest payoff of all in achieving greater *control* of your time and your life is greater *freedom*.

3. DRIFT, DROWN OR DECIDE

LOOKING UP from her morning paper, Ms. Kay smells smoke and sees the kitchen curtains near the stove in flames. Is the best use of her time to (1) butter her toast and finish reading the news, or (2) do something about the rapidly speading fire? Whether Ms. Kay runs toward the curtains with a pot of water, calls the Fire Department on the telephone, or dashes to the corner fire alarm box, no one would maintain that a better use of her time would be to butter her toast.

Most choices, of course, are not so absurdly easy. After fourteen years in the auto industry, Mr. Williams was considering changing careers. His advancement had been good, but not as good as he had hoped. He found his job as production manager for a Kalamazoo assembly plant only moderately interesting. He was bored with Kalamazoo, and thought that living in Chicago would be more exciting.

Mr. Williams was tempted to make a change. But which? Should he use his production-management experience to change industries? Should he seek a production job in Chicago or some other large city? Should he move first, then find a new job? How should he go about looking? Or should he forget all about production and study to become a real-estate salesman? With so many different options, his final decision is not at all clear-cut.

Like Ms. Kay and Mr. Williams, you and everybody else are faced with all kinds of decisions, some hard and some easy, some large and some small—every day.

Who Can Do It All?

Would you like to be a doctor, lawyer, Indian chief, musician, architect, artisan, baseball player? Would you like to travel to Europe, South America, Nigeria, Timbuktu? It's not just a matter of talent and money. Even an Einstein or an Onassis can't do everything there is to do and see everything there is to see in the world. Decisions, decisions, decisions surround us all, clamoring for attention.

How about today? Will you work, go to a show, read a book, visit friends, sleep late, play bridge? Your time is limited, but your imagination isn't. Most people, in just a few minutes of daydreaming, can come up with enough activities to keep them busy for weeks or even months.

And what about all those things you *have* to do: draw up the report the boss is expecting, answer overdue correspondence, pick up theater tickets, plan your vacation trip, lobby with the personnel man for a new assistant, worry about your son's school grades, go shopping for a new suit, go to the dentist, weed the garden? How can you possibly do everything you ought to do today?

Tomorrow there will be still more things to do. Life is a never-ending stream of possible activities, constantly being replenished by your family, your teachers, your boss, your subordinates, as well as by your own dreams, hopes, desires, and by the need to stay alive and functioning. You have so much to do, but so little time!

Your many options are to some extent a recent development. In the not-too-distant past, when choices were fewer, life and its tools less complex, horizons more limited, people had less need to think about how they spent their time. For all but a privileged few, necessity dictated many actions. Other aspects of people's lives were determined by such fixed conditions as tradition, religion, social class, or where they happened to have been born.

Today, with social, economic, and physical mobility a reality for so many people, and with considerable leisure time available, the opportunities for and pressures of making choices have multiplied. The choices are often complex and difficult. This is especially true for women, who face a veritable explosion of new options.

Everyone Wants Some Of Your Time

Maybe you're at one and the same time a breadwinner, spouse, family member, bridge player, churchgoer, Lion's Club member, and a politically alert citizen. You must juggle the time demands made on you in each of these roles. Nor is that all. A dozen irate customers all demand immediate delivery of the same out-of-stock widget. All the family members clamor for your attention when you come home from work. Three television networks want you to watch their programs. You could spend a great deal of time reconciling these conflicting demands and trying to keep everyone happy.

Some demands by others should be accepted graciously. When something is important to someone you care about, even if it's not important to you, remind yourself that you live in an interdependent world and this means sharing your time to some extent.

After all, you knew when you "hired out" to work for your organization or when you married that you'd be giving up some freedom to decide how to spend your time in exchange for other things you consider important—love, security, companionship, money, dinner. Face it. Sometimes you've got to do what others want you to do. But not always!

Doing What You Want To Do

In discussing her son's future with friends, Mrs. Reed was quite emphatic about the best use of her son's time. After Jack graduated from high school he would go to college at his parents' alma mater. Jack had other ideas. He was tired of school, had doubts about the usefulness of formal education, and felt that the best use of his time would be to travel for a year or two.

What is the best use of Jack's time? The answer isn't clear, although certainly Mrs. Reed and Jack each have rather strong opinions on the subject.

Who is the decisionmaker? Jack is. Mrs. Reed may claim to have the right to decide, but even if Jack does go on to college (if only to please his mother), he has decided.

Situations in which you feel other people are making your decisions for you are not uncommon. A parent, a child, a spouse, a boss, a friend may seem to have as much say about how you spend your time as you yourself do—and sometimes more.

That feeling may be understandable, but the fact is otherwise. Ultimately, another person can only recommend what you ought to do—you and you alone make the final decision. You either accept or reject the recommendation. Of course, some decisions involve painful consequences. Your boss wants you to work on a certain project but you have your own ideas about what you should be doing with your time. If you continue to press your position, you may find yourself without a job. But in many situations the element of free choice is quite large indeed.

True enough, it may sometimes seem that you have little free choice. It is foolish to deny that age, education, background, economic status, sex, and race impose real limits on us all. So let's recognize at the outset that in everyone's situation there *are* uncontrollable elements. It saves a great deal of time to make a realistic assessment of what these are, and then accept them. Playing the game of wishing *"If, only* I were younger . . . or richer . . . or poorer . . . or smarter . . . or more successful . . ." is *not* a good use of one's time (though you may decide that *doing* something about these things is an excellent use of your time).

There are constraints on everyone that make free choice impossible in all situations. But you are free to choose much of the time. Maybe you are kidding yourself if you believe outside factors are controlling your life. It could be you are not even doing a very good job in those areas where you *do* have control.

Are You Clinging To The Past?

Consider the case of one of my clients, a top salesman who was so successful selling his company's products that he was promoted to sales manager. He was proving to be much less successful in his new job, and came to me in desperation. His problem soon became apparent. Upon his promotion he faced a conflict between the old habit of doing the selling himself and the new necessity of training and motivating his salesmen to sell for him. Too often he was answering the question, "What is the best use of my time now?" as if he were still a salesman rather than a sales manager.

The sales manager found that by consciously keeping track of the number of hours that he spent in the old and new roles he gradually was able to change his habits and channel more of his time toward his new responsibilities.

Role adjustments are required whenever there is a major change in your life: going away to college, getting married, having children, changing jobs or localities, retiring. You want to be sure you are making time choices that are right for your current rather than your past situation.

Why Deciding Is So Difficult

At times everybody is faced with wanting to do different and contradictory things. Rational, emotional, and physical needs must all be satisfied, but cannot always be satisfied at the same time. Sometimes they have to fight it out. Work or play golf? Read your book or play with your child? Have a second cup of coffee at lunch or go back to the office? How to decide?

Mr. Smith knew that the use of a dictating machine would save him time, but he hated talking to a blank wall. Should he listen to his *rational* part and save time, or to his *emotional* part and dictate to his secretary? Mr. Smith thought he had solved the problem by putting a picture of his secretary on his desk when he dictated. This gave him the feeling he was talking to a real person who would transcribe his dictation. Everything worked fine until one day his wife visited his office to pick him up for dinner and discovered his secretary's picture on his desk. You can imagine the price Mr. Smith had to pay when he picked himself and the broken picture up off the floor. Perhaps Mr. Smith would have done better to put a picture of his wife and family on his desk to remind him where the money he earned went.

Another kind of conflict makes it hard to choose: long-term vs. short-term goals. Should you cook tonight's dinner or get ready for a weekend dinner party? Water the lawn or read your gardening books?

Mr. Martin had a large backlog of work. To catch up he needed at least a month, yet management demanded there be no more than a week's backlog. Mr. Martin had figured out a procedure that would cut the processing time of each item in half, but his new system would take at least two months to implement.

Should Mr. Martin tell everyone who knocked on his door for their order to come back in two months? This would give him the time he needed to implement the new procedure. But the back-order situation would be approaching chaos.

Or should Mr. Martin keep struggling to get out the work as best he can, keeping at least some people happy as their finished work comes off the production line each day? True, it would take him longer to fill each back order, but that was the way it had always been done. And he would be showing daily progress on the backlog, something he couldn't do if he devoted his energies to instituting the new procedure.

Should Mr. Martin emphasize the short term, and keep some work coming out daily—or the long term, and revise the procedure? Whatever he does, he's going to make some people unhappy. If he takes the short-term route, he loses long-term benefits. If he chooses the long-term route, he gives up short-term value. In a situation like this he might put the decision up to his boss; or decide to take either extreme; or devise some middle-of-the-road compromise, getting out some work daily but also moving the new procedure ahead a little each day. Whatever he does, he needs to resolve the conflict between the short term and long term if he wants to retain his job and his sanity.

Making Decisions

Your time use is the result of hundreds of thousands of big and little choices made each year, month, week, day and minute deciding what to do and how you should do it. Are you aware of the reasons why, for example, you make certain social decisions? Here are some possibilities:

1) *Habit*. For years you've gotten together with the Joneses once a month. You're beginning to lose interest and have to admit that you haven't had such a good time lately. Still, it's such an automatic routine that you continue to go out with them.

2) *Demands of others*. Your husband keeps nagging you

to invite over a couple who might prove to be helpful to his business; finally you give in although you do not like them.

3) *Escapism.* You sit at home and daydream about how nice it would be to get together with another couple you recently met, but you never quite get around to inviting them over since you are scared off by the possibility that they might think you are presumptuous.

4) *Spur of the moment.* You suddenly decide you want to go to a show that evening, phone the Andersons to join you, but find they are already engaged, so you settle for going with another couple you don't like nearly as well.

5) *Default.* You wait for other couples to invite you out, and therefore spend most of your time either at home or among people you might not prefer.

6) *Conscious Decision.* You sit down with your husband, lay out a program of inviting over new acquaintances with whom you have a lot in common and old friends you haven't seen often enough lately.

Spur of the moment decisions can be fine. Nor is there anything "wrong" with decisions that come about by default, the demands of others, escapism or habit. But if you are not satisfied with the payoff from those decisions, more conscious efforts are called for. How tempting it is in difficult situations to drift, dream or drown. But is that really what you want to do? There is an alternative. You can drift, dream or drown—*or* you can decide.

4. CONTROL STARTS WITH PLANNING

"I feel like I waste so much of my time doing things that are not really important to me, while my life is slipping away."

"I have so much to do; there's just not enough time for me to do it all."

"I'm harassed, overworked, tired, tense. I seem to be forever pushing myself, and can't ever relax completely."

THIS IS WHAT I often hear from people who talk with me about their time problems. Behind each statement is a wish that things could somehow be different: "If only I could get on top of the situation." "If only I could be more like so-and-so, who seems to have time to do everything and still manages to be relaxed and happy." "If only I could do what I *really* want to do." "If only I were in control!"

Control starts with planning.

Planning is bringing the future into the present so that you can do something about it now.

Everyone makes plans: what movie to see tomorrow night, which friends to visit next weekend, where to vacation next summer, big plans and little plans, realistic plans and far-fetched plans, playful plans and serious plans.

Most people plan rather haphazardly. They usually do it only when they feel forced to. Perhaps you feel overwhelmed by the work you have to do and this forces you to plan your day. Or you have a large block of uncommitted vacation time and you want to use it in a satisfying way. This kind of occasional, special-purpose planning is a valuable tool indeed, but it does have limitations. If you *only* plan this way you run the risk of not planning when you really most need to.

I have never known anyone who was hurt by too much of the kind of planning I am going to recommend. I have

known many people who have suffered from failure to plan
adequately.

Learning From Professionals

Consider the difference between an amateur and a professional photographer. The person who uses his camera occasionally to capture a birthday party, a scenic view, or a
family outing will snap a few pictures of the cherished moment, eagerly await the outcome, then, often as not, feel disappointed with the results. Out of a dozen or so pictures,
several will come out blurred, one will include only a part of
someone's head, another will capture a frown rather than a
smile. He will rightly conclude he is not a good photographer.

The professional photographer proceeds quite differently.
He shoots several rolls of film. When these are developed he
studies the results, and discovers more bad shots than our
amateur did. But because he has taken so many shots, he sees
some that he is quite pleased with.

Then he goes into the darkroom and considers what he can
do to improve the good shots. He experiments with cropping,
exposure, etc., and he ends up with perhaps half a dozen
prints that he likes particularly well. He selects the very best
of these and, after giving them further careful attention, ends
up with a prize-winning photograph.

These are the differences between occasional and serious
time planners too. The occasional time planner gets a fuzzy
shot of his goal, and may even miss the mark entirely. He's
uncomfortable with the results; they seem hardly worth the
effort. He concludes, and rightly so, that he's not a good
planner, and gives up.

On the other hand, the serious time planner will take many
and frequent shots of his plans. What begins as a fuzzy, ill-
defined jungle of conflicts gradually comes into focus. A wild
shot that does not really represent a desired goal gets weeded
out. The more important aspects of the plan are refined and
elaborated on so that more and more meaning is built into
them.

He checks as the days go by to see how he is following
through on his plans. He looks for problems, false assump-
tions, hang-ups, and difficulties, and makes corrections where

he has to. Like our professional photographer, he makes some readjustments and becomes better and better at what he does.

A banker I know has his work time under control and now spends more time with his family on his boat. By planning his time carefully he's found it easier to take on new projects and adapt his day-to-day routine to fit his long-term plans. He is a good time planner not because he started out that way but because he put time and effort into refining his plan.

Do You Know How You Set Your Priorities Now?

Planning and making choices are often hard work. They involve careful thinking and decision-making. They also force you to recognize what criteria you use in setting priorities. The wife of a very talented filmmaker said during our consulting session that she felt she was wasting her time. Her criteria in setting time priorities, it turned out, revolved around her family's needs, when what she really wanted to do was structure her time in terms of her own needs. She came to realize that once she took care of her own time needs she would feel more comfortable coping with the needs of her family.

Different criteria may result in different priorities and cause a conflict of interests. However, if you're aware of this, as the filmmaker's wife was after our consultation, you'll be better equipped to deal with the conflict. For instance, a teacher may be studying for an advanced degree at night. She cares about her students, but she also wants to better her professional standing. When she comes home from her own classes at the university, should she work on grading her third-graders' compositions or drag out that Comparative Lit. paper she's been writing? If her criterion is her own students' needs, then she grades the compositions, but if her criterion is her own advancement, then a better use of her time is to work on that Comparative Lit. paper. Her choice depends on her priorities; whatever she decides, proper planning will enable her to recognize that she should settle the conflict between her own needs and those of her students.

Many people seem to have difficulty planning because they regard it only as "thinking"—which all too often translates into either "staring into space" or "daydreaming." They need a way to make a more concrete task out of planning. From experience with thousands of people I have concluded that it is much better to conceive of planning as "writing" than as "thinking."

The following chapters contain a number of exercises, and I'll ask you to write the answers to some questions. Writing the answers down will reduce your tendency to daydream, and also help you make better decisions. I call the time when you plan "Decision Time," because that's what planning is all about—making decisions as to *what* and *when* and, if necessary, *how*.

In all planning, long-range, middle-range, or short-range, you (1) make a list, and (2) set priorities. All the items on a list are not of equal value. Once you have made a list, set priorities based on what is important to you now. In my opinion, no list is complete until it shows priorities. Whenever you make a list, finish the list by setting priorities.

It's as Basic as ABC

Use the ABC Priority System: write a capital letter "A" to the left of those items on the list that have a high value; a "B" for those with medium value; and a "C" for those with low value. As you do this, you know that to some extent you're guessing. You're not sure you'll be right on the value. But comparing the items to one another will help you come up with the ABC priority choices for every entry on the list.

Items marked A should be those that yield the most value. You get the most out of your time by doing the A's first, and saving the B's and C's for later. Taking account of the time of day and the urgency of the items, you can break them down further so that A-items become A-1, A-2, A-3, A-4.

ABC's are relative, depending on your point of view (remember, you are the decisionmaker). A task might be an A-priority while you're thinking of all the rewards that come when it is done. But halfway through, when the going gets rough and you don't like the discomfort involved in sticking to it, you drop it in the middle. Was it an A or not? Even so, if you doubt your judgment, whose is better? I say you are the best judge of your own priorities, and if you are not satisfied with the way things come out you need to improve your ability to focus on what you really consider important.

The ABC's are also relative depending on what's on your list. The A's generally stand out clearly in contrast to the less important B's and C's. In a work of art, attention-getters including vivid colors and foreground details stand out from the background and catch the eye first. Your A-items should be the attention-getters on your list.

ABC's may change over time. Today's A may become tomorrow's C, while today's C becomes tomorrow's A. You need to set priorities continually, considering the best use of your time right now.

ABC's may further vary depending on the amount of time you decide to invest in a particular project. You could probably satisfy the boss with about two hours' work on the report he wanted (you feel it's a C), impress him with about four hours (now it's a B), and make a lot of points if you broadened the question under study and devoted ten hours to solving the more general case (you've made it an A).

A few minutes worrying about Bobby's poor grades might help you come up with some good ideas to improve them, but it would be a waste of time to spend too long on it without getting some feedback from Bobby and perhaps his teacher.

While spending an hour a day playing with your youngster may be an A, spending six hours to the neglect of your husband and house can at best be a B, and spending every minute of the waking day amusing him so that neither the youngster nor you sees anyone else is certainly a C.

Obviously, it's not worthwhile to make a big effort for a task of little value. On the other hand, a project with high value can be worth a great deal of effort. Only good planning will let you reap maximum benefits from minimum time investments.

5. WHAT DO YOU REALLY WANT FROM LIFE?

What are your lifetime goals?

How would you *like* to spend the next three years?

If you knew now you would be struck by lightning six months from today, how would you *live* until then?

It may seem trite to say so, but perhaps you've never stopped to take stock. The basic resource that each person starts with is his lifetime—all the minutes, hours, days, and years that he is alive. It's only within this total framework that good time planning is possible. Which is why I recommend you start by defining your lifetime goals.

I'll soon get down to your minute-by-minute problems of today. But right now a written Lifetime Goals Statement will help you discover what you really want to do, help motivate you to do it and give meaning to the way you spend your time. It will give a direction to your life. It will help you feel in control of your destiny. And it will provide a measuring stick against which to gauge alternate activities as they come along. You'll be better able to balance the many aspects of your life. And you'll reduce unnecessary conflict over how to use your time.

A Lifetime Goals Statement is neither magic nor a cosmic exercise in clairvoyance. There's really very little involved in getting one down on paper. Some people do feel a bit uneasy about it. They feel it's overwhelming. They claim it's embarrassing. Or they feel that a written plan will permit their options and take some of the creativity and spontaneity and fun out of their lives. Let me assure you nothing could be further from the truth. Over 15,000 people in my seminars and consultations have composed Lifetime Goals Statements and I believe each one has come away with a clearer picture of just what he wanted to do with his life. Few of them had written down their lifetime goals before they came to my seminars.

So let me put the question to *you*: What are *your* lifetime goals?

In one way or another, whether you have been explicitly aware of it or not, you have been thinking about your lifetime goals almost as long as you have been alive. However, thinking about your goals is usually quite a different experience from writing them down. Unwritten goals often remain vague or utopian dreams, such as "travel," or "becoming a millionaire." Writing goals down tends to make them more concrete and specific and helps you probe below the surface of the same old clichés you've been telling yourself for years.

You can gain a valuable new perspective by seeing your long-familiar thoughts committed to paper, because you can then examine them more closely. Once they have an independent identity, you can scrutinize them better. They can be analyzed, refined, changed, updated, and pondered.

Also, you most likely will discover goals that are important to you even though you never verbalized them or took them seriously before. This happens because writing requires you to be more specific; aims get narrowed down, because you can't write very many words compared to the millions you have thought in your lifetime. In fact, your selection of what you write down indicates priorities that might surprise you.

If you have never tried writing down your lifetime goals, the following exercise will help you get started. If you have a goals list already, you may find it helpful to update your thoughts using this exercise.

Your Lifetime Goals Exercise

Get several pieces of paper, a pencil or pen, and a watch or clock with a second hand, and set aside about fifteen minutes. Write at the top of a sheet of paper the question, *What are my lifetime goals?*

(In identifying lifetime goals you should recognize that you would get different answers at ages five, twenty-five, and sixty-five. So you should interpret your lifetime goals as the goals that represent the way you see your life starting from right now and from the perspective you have today.)

Now, take exactly two minutes to list answers to the question on your paper. Of necessity, you will have to stay very general and abstract, but you should still have time to take account of personal, family, social, career, financial, community, and spiritual goals. Try to make your list as all-inclusive as you can. Try to get as many words down in the two minutes as possible. During this listing stage you are not committed to any of the goals that you write down, so record whatever comes into your head.

Don't be afraid to include such far-out wishes as climbing the Matterhorn, going to a group-sex party, eating a whole cheesecake, taking the year off, building a retirement home in Italy, chartering a yacht, adopting triplets, losing forty pounds by jogging an hour a day. There's nothing wrong with uncensored fantasies.

After the first two minutes are up, give yourself an additional two minutes to make any changes necessary for you to feel satisfied with your statement of goals at this early general level.

You might identify one or two additional lifetime goals by looking for implicit trends in your current pattern of living. For example, if you diligently read books while commuting on the bus, you may have an unspoken goal of continuing your education. Regular reading of the newspaper may suggest goals of keeping informed and entertained. You'll have a chance to decide later whether or not these are really significant lifetime goals.

The Second Lifetime Question

When you list lifetime goals quickly and without much reflection, you probably include a number of generalities such as "happiness," "success," "achievement," "love," "making a contribution to society," and the like. You can pin-point your goals better by now asking a second question *How would I* like *to spend the next three years?* (If you are over thirty, change the "three" to "five" years.) Again list your answers as quickly as you can for two minutes, then take another two minutes to include whatever you may have missed the first time around on this question.

The Third Lifetime Question

Now, for a different perspective, write down this third question: *If I knew now I would be struck dead by lightning six months from today, how would I* live *until then?* (This means that you'd have only six months to live and would have to squeeze whatever you consider important into your dramatically reduced time on earth. Before you start listing, assume that everything relating to your death has been attended to. You have completed your will, bought a cemetery plot, and the like. Your answer to the question should concern itself with how you would *live* these last six months.)

The purpose of this question is to find out whether there are things that are important to you that you're not doing now or which deserve more of your attention in the next six months. You might continue to live as you do now; or, if you had the money, you might want to quit your job and live it up for the last six months. What *would* you do? Write your answers as quickly as possible for two minutes, then go back and improve them for an additional two minutes. (Don't get lost in thinking about this question—just write.)

If you have read to this point without writing answers to the three lifetime goals questions, I urge you to go back and do it now. This is an important exercise, and doing it will really benefit you.

Working Further On All Three Questions

Now spend an additional two minutes minimum reviewing and improving your goals statements in answering all three questions. You may spend longer if you wish.

In looking over all three sets of answers you may have found that the answers to question 2 were an extension of question 1, and this is desirable. Some people also find question 3 (the six-months question) a continuation of the previous two, but others are jarred into sharp departures from their previous plans because of the sudden realization that their time is limited.

For instance, I probably wouldn't quit my work and travel

around the world. I would try to do as much time-management consulting as I could, and I'd definitely take off more time, but basically I wouldn't change very much because I'm happy in what I'm doing.

Someone else may say, "OK, I'm going to stop where I am and I'm going to eat, drink, and be merry because I'm going to die in six months. I'll travel around the world, I'll use up all my money, I'll do all the things I've always wanted to do." There's no one "right" answer. The choice is up to the individual.

For those who are happy doing what they are doing, the six-months question represents an affirmation; they'll continue along as they are.

For those who come up with a completely different set of things to do, some real changes may well be in order. They shouldn't put in good time after bad. The six-months question will help identify some things they would do if forced by circumstance to take stock of their lives. The point is: With proper time management, there's no real reason why they shouldn't start doing most of their preferred activities today.

Now you have a list of goals. But you have probably thought of more to do than there is time to do it in. This lack of time creates goal conflicts.

Conflicts among various goals on your list need not necessarily be disturbing. A goal to spend more time advancing your career may conflict with a goal to spend more time with your family. This competition for your attention can stimulate you to increase the quality of the time you spend on each. If, on the other hand, these goal conflicts cause you to feel frustrated, then a good use of your time would be to try to resolve such conflicts.

How to Resolve Goal Conflicts

Goal conflicts are resolved by setting priorities. You must decide which goals are most important to you at this time.

Some conflicts will seem to take care of themselves when they are put down on paper. If an individual finds that he doesn't assign a high value to what he had long thought he most wanted to do, then chances are he really knew all along that other goals had higher priority. He simply hadn't faced the reality before.

Other conflicts are much more difficult to resolve. If you are faced with a painful choice between two opposing goals, keep in mind that priorities can later be adjusted and readjusted *ad infinitum*. Your goals are written on paper—not carved on marble tablets.

If you are reluctant to set a higher priority for one goal (say, going back to school) and hence a lower priority for another (family time), you could consider each equally important. If you then allocate more hours to one than to the other, you can still tell yourself that they are equally important. Even if they are mutually contradictory, or need to be done in the same time period, you can console yourself by telling yourself that you're giving up one—but only for right now. Next week or next year you will give the other goal its turn.

There is no other way. You must face up to the challenge of deciding what is important to you now by setting priorities. Here is how to sort things out, using the three lists you have already prepared.

How to Set Lifetime Priorities

Take your Lifetime Goals list in hand and spend one minute selecting your top three goals. Label the most important of these A-1. The second most important is A-2. The third is A-3. Do the same for your three-years list, and your six-months list.

At this point you have nine goals culled from the three lists. To pick out the three most important long-term goals of the nine, write on a fresh piece of paper, "My three most important long-term goals are. . . ." Then write them in order: A-1, A-2, A-3. You have now finished a preliminary Lifetime Goals Statement. You have zeroed in on just what it is you want to do with your life as you see it at this time.

When I work with individual clients I spend a lot of time helping them refine their Lifetime Goals Statements. We might go through six or seven drafts over a period of two weeks before we come up with a statement that represents

the client's true preferences. You too will find it helpful to attempt refinements of the statement several times.

Just as a photographer may shoot and reshoot the same
scene to get the desired effect, your Lifetime Goals Statement
will benefit from successive "shots." So tomorrow repeat the
Goals exercise and compare the results. You won't get precisely the same answers, and the odds are you'll come up
with additional information that you didn't include the first
time around. That's just the way the human mind works.

Since the Lifetime Goals Statement is not static, it should
be revised periodically. A good time every year to reevaluate
your statement is on your birthday. Even if you snapped the
perfect picture last year, this year you are different and last
year's picture is not an adequate representation of how you
see things. Your lifetime goals statement should grow as you
grow.

6. GET STARTED RIGHT NOW

THE LIFETIME GOALS STATEMENT helps bring your future into the present by giving you a clearer view of what your ideal future looks like. The second tool for planning your time continues where the Goals Statement leaves off. It helps you decide on specific activities that you can do now to help you achieve your long-term goals.

You cannot *do* a goal. Long-term planning and goal-setting must therefore be complemented by short-term planning. This kind of planning requires specifying activities. You can do an activity. Activities are steps along the way to a goal. Let's say you desire security. Putting $10.00 in the bank or talking to your stockbroker about your investment plans are activities that will move you toward your goal.

When you have planned well on both long-term and short-term levels, then goals and activities fit together like well-meshed gears. Most if not all of the activities specified in short-term plans will contribute to the realization of the goals specified in long-term plans.

How to List Activities Toward Your A-Goals

If you wish to accomplish such goals as happiness, success, or financial independence, an immense number and variety of actions are of course possible. Suppose you just want to enjoy yourself tonight. I bet you could list twenty-five or fifty ways to do it without even including anything fattening or illegal. The same is true of any goal, no matter how crucial or trivial.

To determine the right activities for achieving your A-goals you must (1) list the possible activities for each A-goal, and (2) set priorities to allow you to select the most effective activity to do *now*.

In listing activities, be as imaginative as possible. Quickly write down as many ideas as you can—it's a good way to get creative juices flowing. Trying for quantity *and* speed will allow your intuition to operate. Your perceptions will come directly, unfiltered by your reasoning processes. Also, the pressure of having to list activities will crease new insights. The speed also allows you to run right past your inhibitions, because you simply don't give them a chance to operate. The important part of the Listing Activities exercise is to keep writing. You're wasting your time if your pen or pencil point is not moving across the paper.

Do not make any attempt to evaluate or censor your ideas yet. This list is for your personal benefit only. If you attempt to hide anything, you'll be fooling only yourself. It's important not to characterize activities as "good" or "bad" or "frivolous"—at least not while you're listing them. We'll catch the less significant activities later when we prune the choices.

Also, don't handcuff yourself by the thought that you might not be able to do a particular activity. It may turn out, upon analysis, that you can do an activity even if at first blush it seems difficult or impossible. Just reserve judgment for the present.

And don't let the fear bother you that once you list an activity you will have to do it. No one is going to force you to do it. When you set priorities you may decide that the required time and effort indicate that the activity is not worth the time and effort required. But even impossible dreams may have some future usefulness.

If you run out of activities to list, you might try repeating a previous entry. Try variations on a theme, reactions to previous entries, extensions, additions, implications, reactions, greater or lesser detail, broader or narrower focus. The important thing is to keep writing!

Suppose your goal is to become an expert mountain climber. List all the mountains you might climb in order to achieve your goal, including the seemingly impossible dreams: the Matterhorn and Mount Everest. Perhaps your interest lies in conquering only North American peaks? European? Asian? Breaking activities down by categories, sub-categories, and sub-sub-categories can help. The important thing is to keep writing.

While I've encouraged you to list as many activities as you can without censoring or inhibiting the responses you put on paper, I do have one caution: Don't confuse goals with activities. Remember, an activity is something that can be *done*. Your goal might be to live a healthier life. The specific activities that might contribute to this end could be not eating dessert tonight, exercising three times this week, and giving up smoking for twenty-four hours.

Now you're ready to make your list. Take three fresh sheets of paper and write one of the A-goals selected earlier at the top of each. We're going to break your goals down into do-able activities. Keeping in mind the above instructions, spend three minutes making as long a list as possible of activities that could conceivably contribute toward achieving the first A-goal. Then spend three minutes each to list activities for the second and third A-goals. Go back over the three lists of activities, spending a mininum of three minutes on each list, adding, deleting, consolidating, refining, and even inventing further activities. Identify as many activities as you can.

Let's take the case of a high school sophomore who wants to be a professional baseball player. This is an A-goal for him. But he also wants to go to college, another A-goal. And he has a third A-goal that is more immediate: He wants to be the starting pitcher on his varsity team. The latter A-goal is most immediate. To accomplish it he'll keep in shape through the winter, running a mile every day and throwing indoors in the gym three times a week so that he'll be ready when spring comes. To make sure that he'll be accepted by the college of his choice (let's say USC, which has always had great baseball teams), he'll keep up his studies. Preparing for an important math exam this week is an A-activity. And, of course, putting forth his best effort in a championship game is an A-activity toward his A-goal of being a major-league ballplayer.

A classic example is the woman who wants to return to work. Her three children are now in school and she has some free time. She worked as a nurse before her marriage twelve years ago. To reach her A-1 goal of returning to work she has a number of A-activities she can do: taking refresher courses to help her catch up on what's been happening, talking with other nurses about recent developments, making sure that she's satisfied all the current requirements, seeing what openings are available and how they fit into her schedule.

Another good example is a person who is just graduating from college. His long-term goals include living a happy life and earning a comfortable income. But there's also the shorter-term goal of finding the right career. And that comes down to finding a job. The A-activities for now include deciding what occupational areas to look into, talking to people in various fields that interest him, preparing a résumé, writing letters, making a selection, and finally going to and scheduling interviews.

One client I had felt he was wasting an enormous amount of time. He said, "I'm very unhappy in my job. I'm an insurance salesman but I really feel I belong in public relations. I'm busy looking for a job every coffee break I get, and each lunchtime I'm on the telephone calling people and telling them what I'm looking for."

It turned out that he had talked to five people in the past month, and those were the same five people he had talked to the month before. In short, he was getting nowhere fast. To find a new job in a competitive field like public relations he might have to contact fifty people a month, at a minimum. He should continually be trying new people as the old people did not pay off. This was his A-activity.

Eliminate Low-Priority Tasks

If you were conscientious in listing lots of possible A-activities you should now have too many activities and not enough time for all of them. The time has come for you to set priorities: to switch from being creative and imaginative to being practical and realistic. The way to start is by spotting and eliminating low-priority items.

For each activity on each list ask yourself: *Am I committed to spending a minimum of five minutes (or less if it can be completely finished in less time) on this activity in the next seven days?* If the answer is "no," draw a line through the activity.

You don't have to offer any particular reason for crossing an activity off your list. You may not feel like doing it. It may depend on someone else who cannot help you in the next week. It may be too hard. Perhaps you're too busy this week. Leave only what you are committed to starting for five minutes (and possibly finishing) in the next seven days.

If you have eliminated almost everything from your list, go back, taking as much time as you need, and come up with at least four items you consider meaningful and which you will put time into in the next week.

Don't be concerned about eliminating large or important items (like getting a new job) from your list. If you don't want to tackle it now, draw a line right through the item so it doesn't clutter things up. You can consider it again next week.

After you've pruned all three A-goal activity lists, combine the results into one list. This list will contain perhaps a dozen or so activities that are important and that you are willing to put time into during the coming week. The next step is to set priorities. Classify the most important activity as A-1, the best use of your time. Other A-activities should be numbered accordingly A-2, A-3, A-4. With these priorities in mind, set deadlines for the various activities and schedule them into the next seven days. If you go to a night school class three evenings, that leaves only two weekday possibilities to have dinner out. Which day will it be? And if you are going to start reading *War and Peace*, when will you start? Perhaps commuting on the train to work? Make a note of such decisions on your list.

Pick a Priority for Now

How can you move closer to your lifetime goals? Each day provides a fresh opportunity. Select at least one A-activity to work on right away and do it. You now have the beginning of an action program for achieving your lifetime goals.

Initially, when you select the A-activity to work on each day, make it as short and as feasible as possible. If the A-activity you have selected seems too overwhelming, divide it into smaller segments, then begin with the easiest part, or the one that involves the least problems, or the one you value the most.

Once you've singled out and defined this one task, you've given yourself a clear priority for the day. In the sixteen hours or so that you're awake each day, you can find a few minutes to work toward fulfilling an important lifetime goal. How about starting now?

The Lifetime Goals chapter and this chapter are fundamental to good time management. For quick review, here are the essential points: (1) List possible long-term goals; (2) set priorities for now and identify A-goals; (3) list possible activities for A-goals; (4) set priorities and identify A-activities for now; (5) schedule the A-activities; (6) do them as scheduled.

7. HOW SCHEDULING HELPS

IF YOU FELT overwhelmed before, you may feel doubly so now that you already have added the A-activities for now to whatever else you have been doing already. Presumably, you still want to do everything you did before (wash the dishes, go to work, shop), but now you want to do even more (the A-activities you identified in the previous chapter).

To find a way out of this dilemma put your lifetime goals in the background for a few minutes and start at the other end of the time scale. *What do you have to do today?*

Obviously, you need time for essential activities such as eating and sleeping, and while the amount of time you allocate to them may be variable, there are minimums necessary for normal functioning. Unless you are independently wealthy or have someone to support you, you will have to work to bring in money for food, clothing, and housing. This means dressing, grooming, commuting, and being on the job—all necessary and all time-consuming.

Then you need time for routine tasks: getting out of bed in the morning, reading the morning paper, opening the mail, going to weekly staff meetings, keeping your work area orderly, watching television, washing dishes, chauffeuring the children. The routine tasks are determined by your position in an organization, family ties, civic responsibilities, social obligations, and the like.

Essential activities and routine tasks are everyday motions that you don't normally think much about, and yet they fill up much of your day. In fact, they can easily preempt your life!

One secretary complained to me that she never had time for special tasks that her boss wanted her to do and that she particularly enjoyed. After our discussion she realized the trouble: She spent her whole day on routine duties the boss had asked her to do the day she was hired—answering the

43

telephone, taking dictation, doing the filing, showing people into the office, answering questions, maintaining the stationery inventories. Her routine work load was so heavy that she wasn't able to absorb fun assignments. This is often true of homemakers, also.

Recognize that you may be doing all you can by working very hard and conscientiously just to keep up with these routine tasks—if that is your choice.

Today's tasks are also preordained to some extent by what is already in process: whatever got started yesterday, last week, or last month. It includes activities scheduled on a regular basis as well as commitments for which you have made special appointments. A celebrated author who was an overnight success with his first book received many invitations in the year following his acclaim. Even though he would have loved to have a free day to spend with his family, or to begin work on a new book, he was committed months in advance to speeches, lectures, and TV appearances. On any given day he couldn't decide to sleep late or stay home and read a book. You too may find much of your time taken up by commitments made long ago.

Unexpected interruptions and crises make still further—and often annoying—demands on your time. You wake up to discover you left the headlights on last night and the battery is dead, so instead of getting into the office fifteen minutes early to catch up on some of your work, you find yourself arriving two hours late. You learn that Mr. Jones has called five times to complain that the gizmo you promised him yesterday still hasn't arrived, so you have to rush around like mad to expedite delivery.

Essential activities, routine tasks and previous commitments coupled with interruptions and crises, can wipe out anybody's dream of having a few minutes to pursue a lifetime goal. But they don't have to wipe it out. It all depends on how well you recognize (and deal with) these inevitable time-consumers and whether you are prepared to make time for yourself. I know of no other way: To increase the likelihood of accomplishing important lifetime goals, you've got to plan your time each and every day.

"Who's Got Time for Planning?"

No matter how busy you are, you should always take the time to plan. The less time you feel you have to spare, the more important it is to plan your time carefully. Spend only ten minutes at the beginning or end of the day planning, and it will repay your efforts many times over.

Sometimes you will be so busy that you'll feel you really don't have time to plan. O.K., maybe you don't have time to plan *and* do absolutely everything else you'd like to get out of the way. But think about this: By failing to plan, you will free very little if any time, and by failing to plan you will almost certainly fail to discriminate among ABC's. Even if you are confining yourself to doing A's, you still might not do the best A's. Therefore, although you think you never have time to plan when you are busy, you always come out ahead by investing time in planning *anyway*. Yes, I mean it: Exactly because we lack time to plan, we should take time to plan.

Planning is usually done best first thing in the morning or at the end of the day. There are many advantages to planning in the morning when you are fresh. You gain momentum as you go along. Having just thought about what you have to do, you move easily to getting it done. With the day's priorities clearly in mind you are less likely to be sidetracked as you go along.

The advantage of planning in the evening is that you know where you have come from and this perspective helps you select activities for tomorrow. Also, if you have your day all set when you arrive the next morning, you don't have to debate what to do and consequently waste time. Another advantage is that your unconscious can work overnight on developing ideas so that you arrive at work all primed for action.

The distinctly different benefits of morning and evening planning are both worth taking advantage of. So I suggest you plan in the morning as well as in the evening.

Can you afford the time? I have had several clients keep careful track of how much time they spent on various activities during the week. They were conscientious people concerned about time and planning, more so than the average person. They were convinced of the importance of planning and committed to spending as much time as necessary on it. They found that all of their planning time came to less than four hours a week. They concluded that it really doesn't take long to plan—considerably less than an hour a day—but the results are substantial: more A-1's get done, less trivia interferes. Planning kept them focused on the important things.

Some executives I know have made it a rule not to leave their offices until they have the next day's plan on their desks. A further extension would be to come in fifteen minutes early the next morning and sharpen up that plan. (Of course as interruptions and crises come up during the day, still further adjustments must be made.)

I do almost all my planning early in the morning. As hard as I try, I can't seem to average more than three and a half hours a week at it. I wake up around 5 A.M., before anyone else in the house, and I put this quiet time into my most important activity—planning.

Every morning as part of my planning effort, I look at my Lifetime Goals list and identify specific A-activities I can do today to move ahead toward those lifetime goals. The rest of the time before breakfast I spend doing A-activities. Finishing this book is one such activity and a lot of this work got done before my family got up.

I recommend using Friday afternoon for reviewing the week, planning the following week's projects in a general way but those you'll do on Monday in detail. Use Monday morning for refining your plan and starting your A-goals of the week.

How to Block Out A-Time

One of the main planning tools I emphasize is scheduling. But scheduling means more than just fitting into the hours available all the things you *must* do: meetings, appointments, deadlines. It means also making time for what you *want* to do—your A's.

In laying out a weekly schedule the key is to block out time for the A's that require a lot of time. Schedule large-enough blocks of time to build up momentum. Reserve particular days of the week (say, Tuesday and Thursday mornings) for major projects. Even if your day is fragmented by interruptions, you can still attempt to keep blocks of time intact for the high-value A's.

To find more time for the A's, set aside a special A-time each day and firmly banish all C-items during this period. To create a block of time for A's to get done, start small and allocate, for example, fifteen minutes each day to use exclusively for A-items. You can gradually increase this time for the A-items as you grow more comfortable with the idea of putting first things first.

Try blocking A-time horizontally on a weekly calendar—at the same time each day, say, Monday through Friday, 9:30-10:30 A.M. You can also block vertically down the page—say reserving Wednesday afternoon from 2-4 P.M. as A-time for this week's A-project.

One husband, whose wife was in the habit of accepting many dates for them to go out and who felt he didn't have enough time to be alone with her, went through her calendar and wrote "busy" alongside all the Tuesday nights. When she was asked out for that date, she looked on the calendar and found that she was "busy." He thus freed A-time to spend alone with her.

I've read articles in management literature suggesting that the way to get hold of your time is to record what you do every minute 24 hours a day, 168 hours a week. I emphatically disagree with this approach; not only is it time-consuming and burdensome to keep track of all your time, but I'm convinced that it's a *waste* of time. Suppose you feel the need to make a change in your eating habits. You already know intuitively that you ought to reduce the quantity of fried foods and add a little more protein and a few fresh vegetables to help balance your diet. It would be a waste of time to keep track of every single item you eat before deciding what to change. On the other hand, keeping a daily record of the fried foods and vegetables you eat during a month can significantly help you decrease the fried foods and increase the vegetables. You immediately gain the benefits of better health, and you're freed from the drudgery of spending a month keeping track of everything you eat. Likewise with time. I feel it's much better to watch your time selectively, keeping track of particular problem items which you feel are consuming an inordinate amount of time.

In my experience, people who try to report everything find it so hopelessly complicated that they give up in despair within a couple of days without having made any changes. I believe that recordkeeping for sake of recordkeeping has very little value, but that selective recordkeeping for the sake of influencing the way you do a particular task has a great deal of value.

Make a Time Change

Just as you make a diet change, so you can make a time change. If you feel there's too much work time in your life and not enough family and personal time, start quitting when everybody else does and stop working overtime; start scheduling more weekends with your family.

Too much golf and not enough civic activities? You don't need any complicated time-accounting to get you to cut back on the golf. Too much housekeeping and not enough time for creative pursuits? Let the dust accumulate for a day or two.

You don't want to recordkeep but you do want to schedule your time, because you can find a great deal of time through careful scheduling of whatever you really want to do. Remember: *There is always enough time for the important things.* The busiest people are able to find time for what they want to do, not because they have any more time than others but because they think in terms of "making" time by careful scheduling.

Trying to do the same thing at the same time each day both conserves and generates energy. It conserves energy by cutting down on indecision. You perform menial tasks by rote. It generates energy through habit—the habit of expecting to make phone calls, plan the meals, read the paper, attend a class, or go to a meeting—all at a particular time.

You Have Two Kinds of Prime Time

Another very important aspect of scheduling is "prime" time. *Internal prime time* is the time when you work best—morning, afternoon, or evening. *External prime time* is the best time to attend to other people—those you have to deal with in your job, your social life, and at home.

Internal prime time is the time when you concentrate best. I know early birds who never get a good idea after 7 A.M. and night owls who are most creative between 10 P.M. and midnight. If you had to pick the two hours of the day when you think most clearly, which would you pick? From 10 A.M. to 12 noon? From 4 P.M. to 6 P.M.? The two hours that you select are probably your own internal prime time, but during the next two weeks you might check to see whether your concentration really is best during those hours.

Try to save all your internal prime time for prime projects.

Most business people pick the first couple of hours at work as their internal prime time, yet this is usually the time they read the newspaper, answer routine mail, get yesterday's unanswered telephone calls out of the way, and talk to colleagues and subordinates. It's much better to save such routine tasks for non-prime hours.

One housewife experienced a great spurt of energy after her husband and kids left the house. She rushed around madly making beds, washing dishes, doing the laundry, picking up toys, so that by 11 she had gotten all of her housework out of the way. Then she collapsed until 2:30, when it was time to pick up her children at school. Her intentions were excellent: She thought that if she got all her repulsive chores out of the way she would have lots of free time for candlemaking, a part-time income-producing project she enjoyed doing. But she found she was too tired after her chores to do her own-time things. Since she had the house all straightened up by 11, she was also reluctant to take out all her equipment and spread it all over the place and make a mess again. The result was that she felt she didn't have enough time for candlemaking. As an outsider I was quickly able to see that she was making a basic scheduling mistake. The simple change of reversing her candlemaking and housecleaning activities netted her two hours of prime time for her candlemaking project.

The chemical research analyst who spent the afternoon skimming through professional publications for recent developments in his field and completing routine administrative forms was making the same mistake, but he did it in reverse. He was a late starter, and really got going after lunch. When he switched his routine chores to the morning, he had the afternoon free to do the more creative part of his job.

External prime time is when external resources (usually people) are most readily available for decisions, inquiries, and information. It's the time when you can catch the boss for that needed decision before he leaves for a week's business trip. Salesmen recognize that their external prime time runs from 9 to 5—the hours when they meet face to face with their customers. So they schedule routine matters for before or after that period.

It's important to make sure in advance that you're going to be able to see the people you have to. The housewife will have to make appointments to see the dentist, the doctor, and her hairdresser. She knows when the stores she uses for shopping open and close. She's in touch with other mothers about the scheduling of next week's car pool to get the kids to school.

The executive makes sure that when he places a phone call he has a high chance of finding that the person he needs on the other end is available. He has to know when his colleagues are free for consultation—and he should plan to take advantage of that time.

Most people aren't very good at putting themselves into the other fellow's shoes, and therefore aren't very good at thinking in terms of another person's schedule. Yet there are big dividends when you do so. One executive I know spends extended periods with his boss during the lunch hour because he knows the boss rarely goes out. They have a sandwich in the office without being interrupted, since everyone else is out to lunch.

Another choice time to catch the boss might be just a shade after he comes in, as he is taking off his hat and coat and before he has a chance to get immersed in other things.

For Effective Scheduling—Stay Loose

Flexibility is needed to accommodate whatever situation may arise. If you fill up every moment in advance with appointments, without any breaks except for lunch, you are bound to go home frustrated, nervous, and tense.

The unexpected happenings need their time, too. Even with a light schedule in prospect, the incoming mail, visitors, and telephone may put enough demands on your time to create an overload. Experience will tell you that although you may not be able to anticipate specifics, there will be interruptions and distractions during the day that will take up your time. You need some slack time to handle whatever unexpected crises and opportunities come your way during the day.

Therefore, always reserve at least an hour a day of uncommitted time. Leave holes in your schedule for recovery from a long interview, and set aside time enough to read the mail and catch up on paperwork. Try to get absolute musts out of the way early in the day so you will feel less frantic about interruptions and distractions.

Rigidity in setting and following demanding schedules without variation creates the feeling of being regimented by the clock, and living your whole life with a constant eye on the clock can be unpleasant. A proper balance of scheduled and unscheduled time carefully planned and then used well can help you get your life flowing more smoothly with fewer fits and starts.

8. HOW TO FIND TIME YOU NEVER KNEW YOU HAD

MANY PEOPLE "on the way up" allow their family and personal lives to be heavily impinged upon by work demands. Others are so achievement-oriented that they feel guilty taking time out for anything that is not in some way related to their work.

Horror stories abound of men who work so hard that they hardly ever see their families and who end up with ulcers and heart trouble. One study several years ago of successful and unsuccessful executives indicated that many men who ultimately fail had made their personal lives expendable to their jobs.

My experience with clients has convinced me that when executives find themselves on a treadmill they tend to lose perspective of what's important. They spend time unnecessarily on secondary matters and let many important ones go undone. This often tends to be cumulative. The more overtime they put in, the more exhausted—and the less efficient—they become. The answer is not to spend more hours on the project but to work more effectively within the time allotted.

I recall one architect who came to me suffering from too much work and not enough play. He had only recently recovered from a bleeding ulcer and again was working sixty hours a week. His complaint was that he never had time to see his wife and young children. I suggested that he take off at noon on Friday and, since summer was just beginning, take his family away to his favorite spot at Lake Tahoe. He rented a cabin, where he and his family spent each weekend during the summer. Not surprisingly, he fell in love again with his wife, got to know his children, and his health improved. Since he knew that he couldn't make up for low productivity by long hours, he concentrated on getting the important things done in the time he had. He actually got more done than he ever had working sixty hours, even though he shaved more than fifteen hours off that total. As a bonus, he got some of his most creative ideas while he was relaxing at the lake, so his leisure time paid off handsomely. All he really lost by cutting back those fifteen hours was the detailed drafting that he compulsively had felt the need to do himself. He delegated it to a draftsman.

Can you work effectively if you are too fatigued from excessive hours? Probably not. Maybe a better solution would be to quit early, take the afternoon and evening off, and come back the next day refreshed and physically able to work twice as hard.

Get More Done by Doing Nothing

I think you will find that if you arrange things so that you find time to relax and "do nothing," you will get more done and have more fun doing it.

One client, an aerospace engineer, didn't know how to "do nothing." Every minute of his leisure time was scheduled with intense activity. He had an outdoor-activities schedule in which he switched from skiing and ice hockey to water-skiing and tennis. His girlfriend kept up with him in these activities, although she would have preferred just to sit by the fire and relax once in a while. Like too many people, he felt the need to be doing something all the time—doing nothing seemed a waste of time. His "relaxing by the fire" consisted of playing chess, reading *Scientific American,* or playing bridge. Even his lovemaking was on a tight schedule.

For an experiment I asked him to "waste" his time for five minutes during one of our sessions together. What he ended up doing was relaxing, sitting quietly and daydreaming. When he was finally able to admit that emotional reasons caused him to reject relaxing as a waste of time, he began to look more critically at that assumption. Once he accepted the fact that relaxing was a good use of time, he became less compulsive about being busy and started enjoying each activity more. Previously he had been so busy *doing* that he had no time to have fun at anything. He began to do less and have more fun. When I saw him about three years later, he still had as busy a schedule as ever, but he was able to balance that activity with relaxing so that he came back to work

Monday morning not pooped out from a strenuous weekend, but refreshed.

In my opinion, nothing is a total waste of time, including doing nothing at times. Anything can be carried to extremes, of course, and I recall one client who needed to be pepped up from his indifference to any activity. He rediscovered his energy after we sat down with his unpaid bills and figured out how few days could go by before he'd find himself in serious trouble.

Sometimes the only way to get more leisure time is to reduce arbitrarily the demands of the job. If your attempts to get more relaxation don't succeed, you may have to make some basic changes in your work situation. A credit manager for a men's-clothing store struggled overtime for two years. He never could get his boss to let him have an assistant to take over some of the details. He finally decided it was hopeless and found a job with another firm where he didn't have to work eighty hours a week, and had more time to spend with his family. The chief accountant in the same firm solved the same overload problem by deciding to do as much as he could and not worry about what didn't get done. His solution was more successful: When the boss saw that the work wasn't getting done, he let the chief accountant hire more help. The credit manager would have been a lot happier if he had similarly confronted his boss's stubbornness—or changed his job sooner. He could have saved himself two years of misery.

The Homemaker's Special Problem

The homemaker's problem of finding leisure time is particularly acute. The demands go on twenty-four hours a day, and such deadlines as getting a meal on the table or clothes on the family's back are unyielding. Interruptions tend to be traumatic; children get hurt or sick or need emotional help *right now*. Mother stays on the scene all the time. She can't turn off her job at 5 P.M. and come home to find dinner waiting. The truth is that, with purchasing, budgeting, minor repairs, husbandly complaints, family nutrition, keeping inventory, deciding how many kids can wear this sweater or use that bike—on top of the physical labor of it all—a woman is running a tough little business in which the responsibility is all hers.

Given all these problems, a homemaker must work especially hard to find any leisure time for herself at all. The solution gets back to scheduling. She has to schedule time for herself on a regular basis. One homemaker arranged for someone to come in every Wednesday afternoon; she was a theater buff and used Wednesday afternoons to go to a matinee when there was something she wanted to see. Otherwise, she had it free for museum or gallery visits, shopping, or seeing friends.

I strongly recommend regularly scheduled free time for homemakers. If you say, "I'll take off some day or other this week," something always comes up that interferes. But setting aside time on a particular day leads to the expectation of having that time and results in getting the time you want. One homemaker I knew had a standing Thursday evening date with her husband—to get out of the house, be free of the cooking, and enjoy a restaurant meal as well as the relaxed atmosphere.

If a homemaker is on the alert for external changes that affect her time, she can often find extra hours that she has overlooked. One woman had entered an Adult Extension class on "The Changing Role of Women in Society." She had arranged for a babysitter and had gone each Tuesday afternoon for several months. She knew weeks ahead when the course would be over, but she did not make any effort to schedule that time profitably for herself, and so she let the sitter go when the course ended. She could have furthered some other lifetime goals in the time that was open for her on Tuesdays.

I find it a good idea on regular occasions to take a look two or three months ahead and ask what's on tap. What advantage can you take of the time when the kids are in school, or when your associates are on vacation? Note what events will influence your schedule in a major way: the semiannual national sales conference, the deadline for the seasonal catalogue. What has to be done to allow for pickup of activity after Labor Day? For people being away around Christmas? For the seasonable winter blues in February—maybe a weekend in Bermuda or Mexico City?

By taking note of these situations well in advance, you can

often make or find opportunities for furthering some of your most important goals.

Make the Most of Your Transition Time

I've suggested that you need to balance work and play. And again you might say to me, "But I don't have enough time for everything." Well, again I say, "Let's see if we can find some time." More specifically, let's see if you can find some time that you have previously overlooked. One kind of time that is often overlooked is what I call "transition time."

This kind of time starts when you awaken in the morning and ends when you begin your regular day's work. For most people it amounts to about forty minutes a day, usually a bit longer for women than men. One man I know has reduced it to fifteen minutes. He uses the time only to do essentials—eat breakfast, shave, dress—and he does these as quickly as possible.

There may be an advantage in extending rather than reducing this transition time. If your day is broken into many parts, transition time offers you perhaps the only block of time you'll have alone and undisturbed. It is a good time to reflect on the best use of your time during the coming day and to consider those time management techniques that will help you get things done. As I mentioned before, I get up early—5 A.M.—and spend two hours of transition time planning the rest of the day and working on today's activities to further my lifetime goals. What is the right time to wake up in the morning? Almost every time you read about a busy, famous man (Senator Dirksen was one I remember), he started with paperwork at 5 or 5:30 A.M. and had accomplished mountains by the time the phones started ringing at 9.

There are other ways to enrich transition time. The late Robert Kennedy was reported to have listened to Shakespeare plays while shaving. One creative manager, realizing that he got some of his best ideas in the morning, has come to expect them and "catches" them for further development while they—and he—are still fresh. This can also be hobby time for jogging, painting, sculpting, reading, writing, or whatever.

How to Use Commuting Time

If you feel it takes you too long to get to work, have you considered moving closer? In most cases this is not practical, yet more often than you might suspect a person does have the very real option of moving closer to his place of employment. If you're a professional person, how about working out of your house twice a week and skipping that forty-five minute commute on the freeway?

If you drive to work you're limited in the use you can make of the time you spend sitting in traffic jams. Safety comes first. But you can also listen to the radio. You can practice that new vocabulary exercise. More and more cartridge tapes on educational subjects are becoming available, so you might learn a foreign language, listen to a business report, or take a memory course. Commuting time offers a chance to preview and plan your day, though you should crystallize that plan on paper as soon as you sit down at your desk.

How to Use Coffee Breaks

Coffee breaks can be a good time to relax. But suppose you're not particularly tense or tired. How about learning a word from your dictionary? Writing that unpleasant but important note to the bank telling them why your installment payment is late? Or calling your dentist for an appointment before that temporary filling falls out?

The True Price of Lunch

In some selling jobs, of course, the client is crucial, and in such a situation a working lunch may be beneficial. But by and large, a full-scale lunch is a fantastic waste of time. For most people, lunch just adds calories and expenses they can well do without. Many doctors today are dead set against "Three square meals a day," and many first-rate M.D. diet specialists either skip lunch altogether or have some cottage cheese and that's it.

Lunch time offers a great time to get things done while the phones are quiet and others are busy. On the other hand, if you have a hectic business day a lunch break may provide the only breathing time for you. In that event, if you cut back on your lunch time you might decrease your effectiveness the rest of the day. Maybe this is a good time for you to take a walk or a swim at the Y.

A general merchandising manager, recently promoted, no longer took a regular lunch time off. He felt that since his job involved more responsibility, he should be available all the time, and so he just grabbed a quick sandwich on the run. After several weeks of this, he found himself irritable in the afternoon, snapping at his colleagues, and having difficulty concentrating on important matters. I convinced him that he needed a sit-down lunch to restore his energy and inner calm. So he began having a more leisurely lunch and made certain that nothing interfered with this mid-day break. He developed the practice of going to lunch with a different person each day. Some were friends with whom he enjoyed a social occasion. But gradually he also lunched with all his subordinates and got to know them better. When he had to ask them to do something for him or when they were asking him for help, he had the benefit of personal relationships to support those quick back-and-forth requests.

He was careful, even though he took a long lunch time, not to eat too much, as he found it made him sleepy in the afternoon. But as this executive found out, what you eat might not be nearly as important as who you eat with and what you talk about.

How to Use Waiting Time

If you have to wait for the subway, bus, or your car pool, you can use those patches of time profitably, too. You might read the paper, but suppose you've had a lifelong goal of reading the classics. Most of them are available in paperback. You may not always feel like reading *Don Quixote* as you wait for the bus at the corner of Main and Pine, but isn't it nice to have the option?

Waiting time can also help solve that particularly tricky problem that's been bothering you at work. Think it through sequentially. First, try outlining the problem step by step. Then, if you have more time, pick out an aspect that might be thoroughly explored in, say, five minutes. You probably won't be able to solve the whole problem, but at least you have the ball rolling.

Make Your Sleep Work for You

What time should you go to bed? If you decide to get up early, does that mean you should go to bed early? The largest single block of time is sleep time. Are you sleeping your life away? Doctors have found that often many people spend many hours in sleep for which there is no physical need. When these habits are changed and these people try to do with less, they often find no difference in health or efficiency.

You might experiment with reducing your sleep time by, perhaps, half an hour. Give yourself a few days to get adjusted to the new pattern. If you are as effective as you were before, you will gain the equivalent of a week of Sundays in the course of a year.

There is great variation in sleep needs, not only between one person and another, but also for each person. Weekend patterns usually are very different from weekday habits. And if you always stay up Tuesdays because that's your bowling night, perhaps you've noticed that you're not unusually tired the following day.

If you like, you can put some sleep time to work once you realize that most body functions continue while you are asleep. As your dreams show, your subconscious works while you sleep. Why not deliberately put it to work on your tough problems? Here's how:

Pose a question to your subconscious just before you fall asleep. Select one that requires hours of thought—after all, your subconscious will have four to eight hours to work on it. Now, don't waste time thinking about it consciously, but do expect a meaningful answer when you awaken. Many who have tried this method have found it successful. But if it only keeps you awake, by all means forget it.

What do you do if you have to put eight hours a day into a job you don't like? Whether it's for a summer or a year, let's say you have decided to stay at least temporarily in a job that is not satisfying. If you're simply working to bring in money, is there any way that you can do more than just mark time?

I had a fascinating talk recently with a young man who is a devoted fish breeder. He began breeding mollies at the age of ten and has worked his way up to breeding killifish. Probably because of his strong hobby interest—he spends three hours every evening on his fish-breeding project—he has found a very routine civil-service job. While he is filling out forms for the state, he also plans what he's going to do next about his fish. For example, he recently decided to breed a rare species of killifish which had to be imported from Africa. These fish were being imported under the Endangered Species Act, and he did much thinking about how to breed them successfully in his second-floor apartment, quite different from their natural habitat in the African stream. His routine job gave him the money and the free time he needed for his hobby.

Hawthorne is a famous example of what can be accomplished while working in a humdrum job. He spent years at the Customs House in Salem, Massachusetts, and produced four novels, including the classic *The Scarlet Letter*.

How to Repeal Parkinson's Law

I feel that so long as people do the job they are hired and required to do, they shouldn't have to look busy every minute of the time. I have always tried to give the people who work for me a real incentive to make good use of their time by allowing them to do reading, writing, crocheting, or whatever they want, after they finish my work. I have even sent them home early when there was nothing else to be done.

The policy of making people sit at their desks even if they have nothing to do breeds bad time habits and accounts for a certain amount of psychological aggravation. It isn't surprising that work expands to fill the time allowed for its completion, as C. Northcote Parkinson has stated, since all too often there are no alternatives available. I propose that it's time to repeal Parkinson's Law by allowing people to reap the benefits of getting done early and letting them do their personal things.

In "limitless" jobs where there are truly an endless number of things that could be done—such as creating advertising copy, researching, selling encyclopedias, removing every speck of dust from the house—Parkinson's Law theoretically doesn't apply; there is always enough work. In practice, certain tasks tend to be done on a particular day and are then stretched out. You really can't push people to be creative by the clock, and beyond a certain point simply putting in the hours is not necessarily the best way to get creative work done, as the architect I mentioned earlier learned.

Parkinson's Law is real, and work does expand to fill the time available, because you *need* to fill up time when you can't go home early. Try to convince your boss to let you go home if you've finished all your work by telling him what a great incentive it will give you to complete your work quickly. If you're unsuccessful, try to convince him to allow you to satisfy your personal priorities of reading books, writing your own letters, and the like while you handle the switchboard, the service counter, or the reception desk.

Making the Most Out of One Spare Minute

You can squeeze in a start toward your lifetime goals if you are ready to pounce on all the spare minutes as they come along and convert them into lifetime-goal/A-activity time. A very helpful way to do this is to develop what I call "special-emphasis goals" lasting from a week to a couple of months. Each day do something to squeeze in at least one A-activity for each special-emphasis goal.

Let's say your lifetime goals include intellectual development. You decide to improve your vocabulary as a means to improving your intellect. A special-emphasis goal might be to learn a new word from the dictionary every day for a month. It takes only a minute to find a good word, check on its meaning, and think of a couple sentences you can use the word in. Then squeeze that word into your conversation several times during the day.

A budding gourmet cook had a special-emphasis goal of trying a new vegetable dish each day for a week; she laid out the whole week in advance and each day pulled out a new recipe and was quickly on her way.

A married couple, feeling a bit lonely, laid out a program of renewing acquaintances and meeting new acquaintances every weekend for a month. Their special emphasis goals applied to Saturdays and Sundays only. In a month they had eight very pleasant social evenings or afternoons, going out to dinner, playing records together, and talking politics.

Isometric exercises can be squeezed in while you are making dinner or sitting, or even while waiting for another person to answer the telephone. Here again, if you keep in mind your added special-emphasis goal of fitting in some exercise, you will find many opportunities during the day to realize it.

Work goals can be developed as special-emphasis goals. A salesman can go after one big-ticket customer each day. A factory superintendent can personally check the quality of one finished automobile by driving it home directly off the production line. A freelance journalist can clip at least three story ideas every day for those times when he can't think of a thing to do. An office manager can take a couple of extra minutes to become more friendly and learn about a different employee each day. All these activities can be squeezed in when you have a special-emphasis program suggesting *now* is the time to make an extra effort toward realizing a particular goal.

Not only are these A-activities on a special-emphasis goal a practical step toward getting where you want to go; they also become tremendous morale boosters. Daily you see yourself coming closer to your lifetime goals by remembering what you want to do—and doing it.

You don't want your special-emphasis goals to be out of mind because they're out of sight. Write the goal on a letter card and slip it into your pocket as a reminder. Or how about putting up a sign? I suggested to one client that he put a little sign on his desk where only he could see it. It said, "Am I talking on the telephone too long?" He had admitted to me that he generally did talk too long. Putting this reminder by his phone each day for a week helped to reduce his overlong telephone calls.

A homemaker trying to do the least amount of dusting and homemaking possible this week put a sign in her kitchen saying, "Get out of the kitchen and have a good time."

No time? You've got to be kidding!

9. MAKING THE MOST OF PRIORITIES

THE MAIN SECRET of getting more done every day took me several months of research to discover. When I first started delving into better time use, I asked successful people what the secret of their success was. I recall an early discussion with a vice-president of Standard Oil Company of California who said, "Oh, I just keep a 'to-do' list." I passed over that quickly, little suspecting at the time the importance of what he said.

I happened to travel the next day to a large city to give a time-management seminar. While I was there I had lunch with a businessman who practically owned the town. He was chairman of the gas and light company, president of five manufacturing companies, and had his hand in a dozen other enterprises. By all standards he was a business success. I asked him the same question of how he managed to get more done and he said, "Oh, that's easy—I keep a To Do List." But this was a list with a difference. He told me he considered it a game.

The first thing in the morning, he would come in and lay out his list of what he wanted to accomplish that day. In the evening he would check to see how many of the items he had written down in the morning still remained undone and then give himself a score. His goal was to have a "no miss" day in which every single item was crossed off.

He played the To Do List game much as you cover the squares on a bingo card, getting items on his list done during the day as opportunities presented themselves—talking to someone on the phone, bringing up points at a meeting, exploring a creative project in the evening with his wife. He made sure to get started on the top-priority items right away. Toward the end of the day he initiated whatever calls, actions, or letters were necessary to finish up his "bingo card" for a perfect score.

Again and again when I talked to successful businessmen and government administrators, the To Do List came up. So during one of my seminars I asked how many people had heard of keeping a priority list of things to do. Virtually everyone had. Then I asked how many people conscientiously made up a list of things to do *every* day, arranged the items in priority order, and crossed off each task as it was completed. I discovered that very few people keep a list of things to do every day, although most people occasionally make a To Do List when they are particularly busy, have a lot of things they want to remember to do, or have some particularly tight deadline.

Only a Daily List Will Do

People at the top and people at the bottom both know about To Do Lists, but one difference between them is that the people at the top use a To Do List every single day to make better use of their time; people at the bottom know about this tool but don't use it effectively. One of the real secrets of getting more done is to make a To Do List every day, keep it visible, and use it as a guide to action as you go through the day.

Because the To Do List is such a fundamental time-planning tool, let's take a closer look at it. The basics of the list itself are simple: head a piece of paper "To Do," then list those items on which you want to work; cross off items as they are completed and add others as they occur to you; rewrite the list at the end of the day or when it becomes hard to read.

One of the secrets to success is to write all your "To Do" items on a master list or lists to be kept together, rather than jotting down items on miscellaneous scraps of paper. You may want to keep your list in your appointment book. One executive keeps a special pad on his desk reserved for his To Do List. I know one woman who never buys a dress without a pocket in it so she can keep her To Do List always with her.

Another homemaker was forever losing the lists she made. She spent more time looking for yesterday's list than she spent making today's. To help her get control of her time,

I had her put all her lists in a notebook. She had the added benefit of being able to cull undone A's from previous lists.

Some people try to keep To Do Lists in their heads but in my experience this is rarely as effective. Why clutter your mind with things that can be written down? It's much better to leave your mind free for creative pursuits.

What Belongs on the List

Are you going to write down everything you have to do, including routine activities? Are you only going to write down exceptional events? Are you going to put down everything you *might* do today or only whatever you decided you *will* do today? There are many alternatives, and different people have different solutions. I recommend that you not list routine items but do list everything that has high priority today and might not get done without special attention.

Don't forget to put the A-activities for your long-term goals on your To Do List. Although it may appear strange to see "begin learning French" or "find new friends" in the same list with "bring home a quart of milk" or "buy birthday card," you want to do them in the same day. If you use your To Do List as a guide when deciding what to work on next, then you need the long-term projects represented, too, so you won't forget them at decision time and consequently not do them.

Before you even consider doing anything yourself, look over the list and see how many tasks you can delegate. Not just to your subordinates or the babysitter, but to those at your level and even higher, who do a job more quickly and easily, or who could suggest short-cuts you'd overlook.

Depending on your responsibilities, you might, if you try hard enough, get all the items on your To Do List completed by the end of each day. If so, by all means try. But probably you can predict in advance that there is no way to do them all. When there are too many things to do, conscious choice as to what (and what not) to do is better than letting the decision be determined by chance.

I cannot emphasize strongly enough: You must *set priorities*. Some people do as many items as possible on their lists. They get a very high percentage of tasks done, but their effectiveness is low because the tasks they've done are mostly of C-priority. Others like to start at the top of the list and go right down it, again with little regard to what's important. The best way is to take your list and label each item according to ABC priority, delegate as much as you can, and then polish off the list accordingly.

One person I know color-codes the entries, using black for normal entries and red for top-priority items. For people who have trouble living with priorities, I have found that it's helpful to use one piece of paper for the A's and B's and another page for the more numerous C's. The A and B paper is kept on top of the C list, and every time you raise the A and B list to do a C, you're aware that you're not making the best use of your time.

Items on the To Do List may be arranged in several forms. One form is functional: to see, to telephone, to follow up, to think about, to decide, to dictate. Or you can group activities based on the similarity of the work content (everything about water pollution), the same location (several customers in one neighborhood), or the same person (several topics needing the boss's opinion). You can have a single item on your To Do List represent a group (processing the papers in your in-box, doing errands).

Don't Worry about Completing Your List

Now go down your list, doing all the A's before the B's and the B's before the C's. Some days you may get all the items on your list done, but more likely there will not be time to do them all. If you are doing them in ABC order you may not even finish all the A's sometimes. On other days you will do the A's and B's and on other days A's, B's, and some C's. One rarely reaches the bottom of a To Do List. It's not completing the list that counts, but making the best use of your time. If you find yourself with only B's and C's left, take a fresh look at possible activities and add to your list items such as revising your filing system for greater accessibility, finishing *War and Peace,* picking out a birthday present for your aunt—all A's that were in the back of your mind but didn't make it to the original list. With a little extra time, today they can be started.

Many office workers, homemakers, and professional people have come to my seminars because they felt the need to "get organized." Most report a couple of months later that they feel much more organized simply because they regularly list and set priorities. For example, a newly appointed head nurse used the listing/setting priorities approach for her home life after she had found how well it worked at the hospital. Good time use is as important off the job as on it. You don't want to turn your off-work time into a work-like situation, but you can relax even more if those things you have to do are organized with the aid of a To Do List, then gotten out of the way quickly.

The chief accountant I mentioned in the previous chapter spent his time making sure that of all the possible things he could do, he was really doing the most important. He took time to set priorities and went home feeling on top of his job because he had done the most important activities on his list.

If little things mean a lot, a list of things to do in priority order means a great deal because it provides you with the security of knowing that nothing is missing; an affirmation of all your important activities; a motivation to cross off items you don't need to do; and a reservoir from which you can select activities to be done next.

By doing more A's and fewer C's, the hierarchy of your accomplishments will change. You can break up your old A's into new A's and B's, downgrading your old B's to C's and dropping most of the old C's off your list entirely.

How to Do More Things That Matter

For instance, a year ago attending Parents' Day at your daughter's school would have been rated A. But now you're involved in a part-time fashion-design business, and your daughter understands how busy you are and how much satisfaction you derive from your business, so you won't go to Parents' Day unless it's a slow time in your business. Last year you attended to every detail of the annual inventory yourself. Happily, while you were doing it, you recorded the necessary steps so that this year, with that reference guide in hand, last year's A (figuring out what to do) becomes this year's C: following a routine. Now you are able to delegate the annual inventory to the new stock boy and use your time to merchandise your products better.

The salesman who continually upgrades his customers finds that last year's A—the $100-unit customer—is this year's C. Now his A-customer is a $500-unit account; his B is a $250-unit account. He upgraded his business this way by conscientiously going after the A-accounts. He spent more and more of his time with those who bought over $100, so gradually he was able to consider anyone below $100 to be a C. To encourage this continual upgrading, he went through his customer files each week and threw away at least one low dollar prospect or customer. In my experience, most salesmen could benefit substantially by arbitrarily weeding out 20 percent of their customers in terms of present and potential volume.

Learning a musical instrument is much the same. When you first play the piano your A is to practice easy pieces. Once you become proficient, it would be a C to continue playing them. So you practice more and more difficult pieces. When you are learning a difficult piece, the A is to play it slowly but accurately and the C to play it fast with what would likely be many mistakes. As you become more proficient in playing a passage, the A becomes playing the passage at its correct tempo.

In learning and applying time use skills, it may be an A to watch how to spend every five minutes for an hour so that you become much more aware of time use. Once you become automatically aware of time use, it is a C even to think about time passing unless you want to sharpen up that skill again.

The good time user has a constant stream of A's going through the pipeline and is not hung up on which A to do or how to do it or trying to be a perfectionist about a particular A. Rather, he does a number of A-tasks daily and remembers that as soon as he has identified the best use of his time, the time to do it is now.

10. TASKS BETTER LEFT UNDONE

HOW OFTEN HAVE YOU resorted to poking through routine work (to get a feeling of satisfaction because you're doing the processing efficiently) while you let more important activities go because you want to avoid the feeling of doing them inefficiently?

Resorting to desk-neatening and turning out gobs of trivia can provide more *temporary* satisfaction than tackling an important but perhaps frustrating high-value task.

For example, neatening the desk. You would be unlikely to label this as an A-activity unless it's become a disaster area. But because it's such an easy thing to do and the results show immediately, you might very well spend an extra few minutes unnecessarily neatening your desk when perhaps the thing to do is get away from your desk and go out and see what you can do about the personnel problem that needs solving down in department 73.

The harried field representative whose plane leaves in forty-five minutes gives one more instruction to the office help before going on a two-week trip. He is giving in to the urge to do a C which might very well mean messing up the most important A he can do, namely, catching the flight.

Why do people have this strong tendency to get bogged down with C's? One reason is that many activities of top value cannot, by their very nature, be performed well. Part of the value may be that they have never been done before. Examples include: setting up a committee to consider manufacturing a new, highly competitive product; diapering a baby for the first time; learning Chinese; switching to organic cooking; finding something else to do with your evenings besides watching television.

The homemaker who collects another delicious-sounding recipe when she has five hundred untried clippings is giving in to the short-term feeling of a great find but is truly wasting her time because she never gets around to using the recipes she has been collecting. She wastes her time clipping instead of providing her husband and children with the substantial meals that she really wants them to have. She may kid herself into thinking that she is making herself a better cook, but the truth is that she is clipping rather than cooking.

You should not expect to do A-activities perfectly the first time. The problems associated with them are new, untried, unknown, and uncertain. Doing them means taking risks, which, whether calculated or not, will sometimes bring on unsuccessful outcome. An A-1 may appear to be of overwhelming complexity, or too time-consuming; or require reconciling views of people who can't or won't agree.

With all these things going against executing a hard A-1, is there any wonder you look around for something you can do well? One of the things you can do well is clear up all the easy C's And you justify it by saying you are clearing them away so that you will then be free to do the A-1 later.

You have very cleverly set up a situation where you won't leave the house until you empty the garbage, won't do the A-1 until all the B's and C's are out of the way. It becomes more important to do the B's and C's than to do the A-1, because you won't do the A-1 until you get the others done. You are making sure you do the B's and C's by hooking them onto the A-1.

There is a certain luxurious feeling that comes from doing whatever you want without regard to priority or time involved. Since you know you're not doing A's, you can waste time and gain the feeling of doing something well, starting something easy and finishing it, crossing an item off your list, and moving the paper from your in-box to your out-box. But don't kid yourself: it's because you're doing all those C's and *not* because you haven't any time, that you don't get to do your A's.

The 80/20 Rule

When I deal with people who claim they are overwhelmed, one of the best ways I can help them is to have them become more comfortable with not doing C's. But people are often very hesitant to let go of C's; therefore, I would like to suggest to you the following: the 80/20 rule.

The 80/20 rule says, "If all items are arranged in order of value, 80 percent of the value would come from only 20 percent of the items, while the remaining 20 percent of the value would come from 80 percent of the items." Sometimes it's a little more, sometimes a little less, but 80 percent of the time I think you will find the 80/20 rule is correct.

The 80/20 rule suggests that in a list of ten items, doing two of them will yield most (80 percent) of the value. Find these two, label them A, get them done. Leave most of the other eight undone, because the value you'll get from them will be significantly less than that of the two highest-value items.

These examples, drawn from everyday life, should enable you to feel more comfortable about concentrating on high-value tasks, even at the cost of ignoring many lower-value tasks:

80 percent of sales come from 20 percent of customers

80 percent of production is in 20 percent of the product line

80 percent of sick leave is taken by 20 percent of employees

80 percent of file usage is in 20 percent of files

80 percent of dinners repeat 20 percent of recipes

80 percent of dirt is on 20 percent of floor areas that is highly used

80 percent of dollars is spent on 20 percent of the expensive meat and grocery items

80 percent of the washing is done on the 20 percent of the wardrobe that is well-used items

80 percent of TV time is spent on 20 percent of programs most popular with the family

80 percent of reading time is spent on 20 percent of the pages in the newspaper (front page, sport page, editorials, columnists, feature page)

80 percent of telephone calls come from 20 percent of all callers

80 percent of eating out is done at 20 percent of favorite restaurants

It's important to remind yourself again and again not to get bogged down on low-value activities but to focus on the 20 percent where the high value is.

A local political candidate came to me for advice two months before the election. He was the underdog against an incumbent who had been in office for many years. He recognized that he would have to make maximum use of his time to win. But he had accepted many invitations to talk to unimportant groups, and found his schedule hopelessly clogged. Little of his time remained to go after groups with large memberships for crucial luncheon meetings and evening lectures.

He knew he had failed to exercise selectivity in accepting speaking engagements. While he felt that he could not cancel any engagements already accepted, he decided he would be much more conscientious about setting priorities in accepting future engagements. It took him some time to come around to this view, because he felt a great need to bring his message to all the voters. We ran down his list of speaking engagements and discovered that, unquestionably, 80 percent of his exposure was coming from 20 percent or less of his speeches. The 80 percent of his time that was going to low-exposure speeches contributed little to his cause. In fact, they wore him out so that he was ill at ease and exhausted for those speeches that really counted. He recalled that Nixon spent the last days of the 1960 campaign rushing to Alaska, Hawaii, Wyoming, etc., to fulfill his pledge to visit all fifty states while Kennedy concentrated on the larger states that would given him an electoral majority.

By the end of our talk the candidate realized he could get out of several unimportant speeches—they had not been definite commitments—and substitute more significant appearances. The real payoff for his selectivity came when he won the election handsomely.

A wealthy woman socialite accepted too many demands of others. She could always be counted on to do anything from licking envelopes to twisting the arms of congressmen. She felt she wasn't getting as much pleasure out of all these activities as she might, because she was letting other people set her priorities. She needed to recognize that 80 percent of her voluntary activities were unsatisfying busywork, and that the real joy came from a few activities which she felt strongly about.

What we did was sit down and create a massive list of over one hundred activities she had participated in (or agreed to participate in) during the past three months. She then looked at them objectively and developed a profile of her A's: helping political candidates, talking with interesting people, working in the field of conservation, and collecting art. Her B's included charity benefits, work above the clerical level for the parents' group at her children's school. Everything else was a C, including supervising the church cake sale, doing hospital volunteer work, and participating in the women's group of the local symphony.

What she did was to take her courage in hand over the next several months and say "no" to all organizations, people, and activities on the C-list. This gave her much more time to become really involved at the art museum. She even began to do a little research on Oriental vases. She also initiated a very well received reorganization of her neighborhood political club.

When Not to Do C's

One of the best ways to find time for your A's is by reducing the number of C's that you feel compelled to spend time on.

The main question with C's is "What can I *not* do?" Think of the great feeling of satisfaction of drawing a line through a C-item on your To Do List—without even having to go through the effort of doing it! Rather than think, "I have to do this C," get into the habit of thinking, "Maybe I *don't* have to do this C!"

Let's say your To Do List contains "Get the car washed." You have given this a C-priority, but are tempted to take a half hour out and get it washed anyway, just to get it off your mind and off the list. It is much easier to get it off your list and forget about it by deciding it doesn't need to be done at all.

Many C's can be turned into what I call "CZ's." CZ's are C's that can be deferred indefinitely without harm.

Definite CZ's include rearranging a pile of magazines, inventorying the freezer (when you just did it last month and nothing has changed significantly in the interim), mopping the kitchen floor just before the children come home on a rainy day, checking the morning mail when your secretary always brings it in immediately upon arrival. You can probably think of many other items that are too trivial to do, or will settle themselves by the passage of time, or are best forgotten unless there is a demand from an outside source.

Some C's need to be deliberately deferred to test whether they become CZ's. They go through an "aging" period to see whether or not they die a natural death. Such possible CZ's include: watering the lawn when it looks like rain, shoveling the snow when it looks like sun, bundling the newspapers today for recycling when the Boy Scouts probably will be collecting in the neighborhood next week, preparing a meeting topic that probably won't come up.

When I am unsure of whether something can be ignored completely, I make a little note of the item on a 3x5-inch index card and stick the card in a file folder labeled "Possible CZ's," feeling secure that it will come up again some day if its important. Once a month I look through the file folder, and am able to throw most of the cards in the trash, congratulating myself on all the things I didn't have to do.

Many C's can be turned into CZ's without any great trouble and with little loss in value. Other C's, of course, must be done. Even though they are trivial, routine tasks, there is the possibility of great loss by failing to do them. You can make such C's palatable by thinking of the larger context into which they fit. A government employee who spends most of a day answering a trivial letter from a congressman makes sure it is done accurately and promptly, because when you work for the government it's wise not to arouse a congressman's ire. Similarly, the salesman who spends the better part of a morning tracking down a delayed shipment of a $2.17 part for his best customer can keep in mind that 40 percent of his entire earnings last year came from this one customer.

When a C Becomes a Crisis

Some things—such as refilling the gas tank in your automobile—that are C's and capable of being deferred, can develop into crises if put off too long. There is no great advantage in filling the gas tank when it is three-quarters full, but you do save time if you fill it when it is nearly empty, since this reduces the number of times you have to make a trip to the gas station. Needless to say, waiting a little bit too long can be very costly as well as time-consuming if you happen to get stuck on a deserted road with an empty gas tank and no gas station within twenty-two miles.

A word of caution. Putting off buying insurance or making a will, even though you are in perfect health and can't imagine any problems, is certainly not advisable. Nor is putting off such a relatively trivial chore as washing laundry. While dressing for a big Saturday evening party, you might find you have no clean underwear.

Remember: Tasks rarely go from the bottom of the C-pile to crisis proportions without some warning. They gradually work their way up the scale. Let's say you've been asked to submit a routine production report. You have a hunch that this is a C that will die a natural death without your having to do anything about it. Several days later, a follow-up request comes into your in-box. You take the item from the bottom of the paper-work pile and place it on the top. Then a phone call comes in inquiring about the report. You now decide it's a B. When the boss says, "Give me this tomorrow or you're through," it becomes an immediate A and gets done. You can watch the priority of these items change. If you're smart, you will realize that fewer than one in a hundred C's ever becomes a crisis. The best approach is *not* to do all the C's just in case, but rather to watch for the follow-up requests to tip you off to a potential crisis, then nip the problem in the bud.

If you can let the dusting, washing, filing, or checking go one more day, then let it. You will have spent less of your life dusting, filing, and washing. If you continually resist the temptation to do the C's, you can significantly increase the number that become CZ's. Always keep in mind the question "How terrible would it be if I didn't do this C?" If your answer is "Not too terrible," then don't do it.

You Need a C-Drawer

Give the ABC's their place. Rather than let the high-quality A's get buried by the much larger quantity of C's, try reserving a special place on the top of your desk for the A items. Create a special "C-drawer" where the unimportant items can get dumped safely out of the way. If you already have a C-drawer, get yourself a bigger one, or a whole cabinet for C's to be kept out of the way. As a start, try physi-

cally separating your paper work into small A-piles and
B-piles and a much larger C-pile. Re-sort the B-pile into
either the A or C group, and then put the A's in the "A-
place" and the C's in the "C-drawer."

If you haven't cleared your desk for a few months, take
everything off the desk and out of all the drawers, and put it
on a table. Going through it, you will probably find there will
be some A's, some B's, some C's, but there will also be a lot
of useless material that you can toss into the trash can. You'll
know the operation is a success if you have to borrow other
people's trash cans to get rid of your junk.

If, like so many homemakers, you don't have a desk, then
you probably have the same problem as Ms. Jones. She had
one paperwork drawer where she dumped current mail, notes
to herself, items clipped from magazines, her children's
school schedules, notices of meetings and appointments, letters to be answered, coupons, announcements of department
store sales, bills and check stubs, magazine-subscription notices, notes on the History of China course she took at night
school two years before, string, ribbon and a fancy bow, and
birthday cards.

When the time came to answer a letter, she had no alternative but to pull out the entire stack of stuff and search until
she found the letter she wanted. Similarly, at the beginning of
each month she had to search through her whole pile to pull
out the bills she needed to pay. She sought every opportunity
to avoid going into her paperwork drawer. She even delayed
answering important mail because she dreaded the search.

The solution to her problem seems obvious—and it was,
although not to her, because she felt so swamped. I suggested
a file box, which she bought, and one hundred tabbed Manila
file folders. She made folders for recipes, bills, letters to be
answered, letters to save, make-up ideas, stitchery projects,
coming events, children's activities, trips to take, books to
read, and the like. Once she finally got her accumulation filed
away, it was easy for her to take each new piece of paper
and put it in the proper folder. Then, when she felt like writing letters she didn't have to use all the time finding the letters that needed answering. She could go directly to the "letters" folder and begin at once.

No doubt many housewives have some type of filing system. The important thing is to keep the A's separated from the C's. If you have a lot of letters and correspondence, you might want to have separate folders for A-letters, B- and C-letters.

Every Housewife Deserves a Desk

Even better than a cardboard filing box, if you can manage it, is a desk. The homemaker has a great deal of paperwork, and she's entitled to a comfortable place to do it. I have seen interior decoration suggestions for putting a little desk instead of an end table along side of a sofa with a lamp on it in the living room, or converting an unused corner of the kitchen into a paperwork place, using the kitchen drawers for paper storage. I heartily applaud such efforts to find the homemaker a paperwork place to call her own.

The owner of a large clothing store came to me feeling overwhelmed by the quantity of paperwork that came his way every day. He was bombarded with information about new clothing lines, order and inventory forms from the many manufacturers he bought from, advertising and promotion ideas from his advertising agency, local papers and radio stations, and tax and payroll forms. He felt it necessary to open all the mail and examine it himself. In addition, he wrote many memos with ideas for improving the store and its merchandise and salespeople's skills.

He was continually reshuffling these papers, since he couldn't quite decide what to do with many of them. Also, there were so many good ideas that he hated to give any of them up. He knew he wasn't making ABC distinctions, and the pile of papers on his desk was overwhelming him.

I enabled him to solve his problem by suggesting that each day, when the mail came in, he arrange it in priority order with the most important on top, then start at the top of the pile and work down. I had him put all of the B and C paperwork he didn't get to that day in his right-hand drawer. The next day he began with the new mail and, if there was time, reached into the drawer and did some of yesterday's paperwork. Often he would go home sorry that he hadn't gotten to a particular item, and so the next morning he would reach into his drawer and pull out that piece of paper and put it with his "today's" pile. Sometimes he would get a follow-up request for additional material on something he hadn't gotten to previously, so again he would reach into the drawer, pull it out, and combine it with the current mail.

Not surprisingly, 80 percent of the paper he put in that drawer never got worked on. He did, however, take 20 percent of it out of the drawer and process it with the day's work.

When the drawer was full, I suggested he take all of the paper and move it to the bottom right-hand drawer. This worked fine for another three weeks, until the top drawer filled up again. He then went through the bottom drawer and threw away what he didn't need. And he repeated the process about every two weeks, or as he needed to.

Next: The Wastebasket

All along, of course, whenever he saw an opportunity, he threw paper into his wastebasket. Probably most of the papers that he had just taken out of the bottom right-hand drawer could have gone into the basket and never been missed, but he was reluctant to throw away something, so I suggested he take his stuff and put it all in a file folder labeled "C's from the bottom right-hand drawer, September 1-30." When he had another batch of material, it was put in a file folder with the date on it and placed behind the first file folder in a large filing cabinet. At my suggestion, he continued to remove the contents of his bottom right-hand drawer to a file folder, which was then kept for a year. He found it most satisfying to make room for his current folder of C-material by removing last year's folder and going through it quickly, congratulating himself on not having done so many things that turned out to be unimportant. At this point, he felt comfortable tossing out most of the stuff and keeping the one or two pieces of paper that still seemed to be viable. These went in priority order with that day's mail and were recycled to the middle drawer if not done that day.

After a year it became clear that he had kept himself from doing much hard work that would have netted him very little benefit. For instance, his thoughts about sprucing up the shelves where he displayed sweaters were obsolete, since he had taken out the shelves and put in racks. His clipping about how to promote costume jewelry could be thrown away, since he no longer stocked jewelry. His reminder to himself about the inadequacies of the stock boy could be dispensed with, because the stock boy quit a few weeks later.

How to Keep on Top of Paperwork

The truth is that you need never shuffle a piece of paper again. This does not mean that you can stop handling paper. But you can develop a system that will keep the paper where it belongs and keep you on top of it—if you need to be. The system must take into account both incoming and outgoing paper, and what happens to it in between.

Incoming mail should be screened and sorted. For a few days, examine all mail critically. Look for opportunities to eliminate or reduce the volume of paper that comes in. (You might find a series of obsolete reports to be discontinued.) You can then tell your secretary what material to screen out routinely and throw away, what to route to others or file directly.

One executive has his secretary sort his daily mail into "Action," "Information," and "Deferred" folders. The "Action" folder requires, and gets, his immediate attention. The "Information" folder he slips into his briefcase for reading on the train. He keeps the "Deferred" file, which includes his periodicals, in a drawer for spare moments or when he needs a break from concentrating on more substantial matters.

You can encourage faster decisionmaking and get work out sooner by writing informal notes right on a piece of incoming mail and sending it on to the out-box. If you need to keep a record of the correspondence for your file, or want a reminder to check for follow-through, have your secretary make a photocopy.

For correspondence that requires a more formal or lengthy reply, a dictating machine can be your best friend. Those who learn how to dictate a finished product on the first try rave about the time it saves. One executive saves even more time by dictating only key ideas and then letting his secretary construct a letter that accomplishes his purpose.

Only Once, With Feeling!

One of my best rules is "Handle each piece of paper only once." Try not to put down an incoming piece of paper that requires a response until you have fired off that response. It is often easier to think of the right thing to say when you've just received the letter and your first reaction is fresh in your mind. In addition, you save the setup time required to familiarize yourself with it again later on.

Not all pieces of paper lend themselves to immediate and final action. Some papers linger for weeks or months and require many actions spread over time before work on them is complete. In some projects every word counts and polishing each word is a good investment. Sometimes you make better decisions if you put them off and think about them for a while.

Therefore, the more comprehensive rule is "Try to handle each piece of paper only once. If you can't, every time you pick up a piece of paper do *something* to move ahead the project it represents." If you can't take a big step, even the smallest step counts.

For example, one executive might pick up a piece of paper and think, "This represents an unpleasant task. I can't bring myself to do it now, but the next time I pick it up I'll make a phone call and get it started." He has done at least something to move this project ahead by planning his next step. The next time he finds the same paper in his hands, he is not likely to put it down until he has made that phone call.

On the other hand, don't do more than is necessary. One secretary complains that her boss is such a perfectionist that he never gets a letter out in fewer than three drafts, even on the most trivial correspondence. She, in turn, has gotten into the bad habit of giving him drafts that can't be mailed anyway because of errors.

Expect your secretary always to give you a letter ready for the out-box. Before you make any changes, ask yourself whether the time spent will significantly increase its value. As an added incentive against perfectionism, think about how much it's worth to you to have your letter in the hands of your addressee rather than tied up in your office for another revision.

The next time you catch yourself needlessly shuffling papers, remind yourself that the most important things often are not on paper at all. Ask yourself what underlying situation the paper represents and how you would deal with it most profitably if you were on top of your paperwork. Then "do it now."

Coping with Information Overload

Many people also do not discriminate between A's and C's when it comes to keeping up with news in their field and current events in general. Given a limited amount of time, what is the proper mix of reading the daily paper, weekly and monthly magazines, and books? Do you spend an hour a day on the paper, an hour a week on magazines, and an hour a month on anything as heavy as a book? Or do you let the daily and weekly events take care of themselves, focusing instead on monthlies and books by experts and specialists in a particular discipline?

There is no "right" answer to such questions; just what you decide is good for you. All I'm suggesting is that decisions be made consciously and then be acted on. If you decide that it's not worth more than ten minutes a day to read a newspaper, and you find yourself going back to an hour a day, question the validity of your original decision. You may decide to give a higher priority to newspapers.

Many executives complain that they don't have enough time to read books that would be useful to them in their work. On the other hand, they find hours each month to read newspapers. Perhaps it is because newspapers are widely available each day, cost little, and are read as much for entertainment as for news. Books usually require an effort to obtain, cost much more, are considered substantial, and are read "seriously." As a result, most executives read hundreds of newspapers a year and only a few books.

Reading Books Like Newspapers

If you feel the need to read more books for your work, try reading them as you would a newspaper, using the following procedure. Each day have your secretary put one book from a want-to-read (that you've given her) in your in-box. Have her take yesterday's book from your out-box. There is no harm in letting a book go to your out-box unread, since you would probably never have even seen it previously.

When you do pick up a book, start by reading the "head-lines" on the book jacket, where the publisher sets forth what he considers most significant. Then glance through the book quickly, looking here and there for something of interest to you. Give yourself no more time than you would take to read a newspaper.

The manner in which many non-fiction books are written suggests an approach to reading them. The author starts with a message he wants to convey, and summarizes it in a couple of sentences that he keeps in front of him as a guide while writing. He develops this message with the aid of an outline, then expands the ideas into enough pages to fill his book.

Your job in reading a book, even if it has five hundred pages or more, is to find these key ideas and understand their application to your situation. The preface and table of contents, as well as summaries that are sometimes found at the beginning and end of a book, will help you to do this quickly. Read the details only when something really meaningful to you seems involved. In this way you can gain much value from a book in a surprisingly short time.

This method can help you upgrade the quality as well as increase the quantity of books you read. Because more books are at least crossing your desk, you can feel comfortable in setting aside one that has no appeal. On the other hand, with the exposure to a number of different books, you are more likely to come across ones that are worth careful study and will repay an investment of several hours' time.

People soon forget much of what they read. Therefore, even if you did read all details of a book, you would not be likely to remember most of it anyway. If you've ever tried to summarize a book to a friend, you'll probably agree that what you recalled and considered worth passing on were only a few salient points. Since you remember little, it saves time to be selective and read only what is most likely to be worth remembering.

Over the years you may have developed a library of books you have found especially meaningful. Once you may have studied these carefully, but with the passage of time much has probably been forgotten. You may want to use the news-paper-reading method to review such books and refresh your memory of the key ideas.

Sometimes you run across a book that may be useful in

the future. Don't take time to read it now; you will have forgotten the details by the time you need them. Instead, have your secretary keep a note of the book in a special file for later reference. One doctor, who formerly had his office piled high with unread books, and abstracts, switched to a 3x5 card entry for each item and now has some room on his desk to read.

If you feel uncomfortable about the seeming superficiality of this approach to reading books, consider it a way of getting started. Even at "newspaper" depth only, you are giving yourself a chance to absorb some useful new ideas. Moreover, you may find that your business reading becomes more enjoyable because you're now able to read more in less time.

Should You Try Speed-Reading?

Clearly, the faster you read, the more time you save. However, I find that few people who take courses in speed-reading manage to maintain much increase in their reading speed. They can speed-read for a few weeks after the course, but most of them soon revert to their former pace. If you have to do a great deal of reading, it may be worth taking a speed-reading course, because studies indicate that if you read at least two hours every day after taking the course, you'll be able to maintain a higher reading speed.

But I think it's more important to read smarter rather than faster. In other words, cut out the C-reading that is unsatisfying, useless, uninformative, or uninteresting and use that extra time and energy on A-reading (most likely at your former reading pace). Since you won't read as much, it's important to be selective about what you read. If you spend less time reading C's, you'll find more time for the A's.

My wife and I have a hobby of reading aloud to each other. We read about twenty books a year this way. We could sit down side by side and read the same books to ourselves in a fraction of the time if efficiency were our only goal. The reason I tell this story is to reassure you that the most efficient way to do something is not necessarily the best one. It is highly inefficient to read aloud—but a great way to spend time together.

11. ACCOMMODATING YOURSELF AND OTHER PEOPLE

SOMETIMES THE WAY you use your time is bound to make others unhappy. Everybody likes attention. Giving each person the attention he wants takes time. And you can't satisfy all of the people all of the time. If you've decided it's a C to attend all the parents' meetings at your daughter's school, you can expect her to be disappointed when you don't go. If you've decided to give up your weekly tennis game because it's no longer fun, you can expect your partner to be disgruntled. If you've decided it's no longer worth your time to keep training an employee who doesn't seem to be catching on, you can expect him to be upset when you get rid of him. If you postpone delivery of Jones' order to satisfy an emergency request from the Smith Co., you can expect Jones to be annoyed or apoplectic, and this time you might even lose Jones' business for good.

It's a real dilemma whether or not to put aside an A of your own when asked to do something else. It might take a lot less time to do what is a C for you but an A for someone important to you—perhaps your spouse or your boss—than it would take to explain why you don't consider the demand very urgent. On the other hand, you don't always want to do other people's A's at the expense of your own.

You can never do everything that everyone wants—there just isn't time. You must set priorities based on the importance to you of the person doing the asking and the consequences if you don't do what's being asked. If the person doing the asking, or what is being asked, is unimportant to you, you may choose to defer the request (at least the first time around). Some of these requests for action that come your way are soon forgotten or downgraded to C's by the asker and don't have to be done at all.

84

Learn to Say "No"

Sometimes the best solution is to say "No" at the outset. This one word, used promptly, properly and with courtesy, can save you a great deal of time. It's important not to let other people fritter away your time, but when you say "No" you have to make it stick while not seeming ruthless or unfair. And everybody knows how hard that is.

You can tell the other person that you appreciate how important the activity is to him but you are too busy to help him out now. If it makes you feel better, apologize and mention one or two of the A's that pre-empt your attention. Perhaps he will see it from your point of view. He might even apologize to you for intruding on your time.

Some people have a great deal of trouble saying "No." A client of mine, Ms. Filmore, found that she was spending most of her time on other people's priorities. When we looked at the situation together, it was clear to us both that she was saying "Yes" because she was afraid to stand up for her own priorities. Perhaps her trouble stemmed from childhood. Her domineering parents had always limited her actions and told her not only what to do, but when to do it.

As we talked she began to see that her reluctance to say "No" wasn't really fair to others. She realized that she would say "Yes" when there was little hope of her actually doing what was asked. In one instance, she disappointed a very important person who would have made other arrangements if he'd suspected that a "Yes" from Ms. Fillmore meant "Maybe." The realization that saying "Yes," and not delivering, was worse for all concerned than saying "No," helped her solve her problem.

There are other ways besides Ms. Fillmore's to avoid saying "No." The administrative assistant who vows to fulfill a request "Right away" (whether he intends to or not), the colleague who offers sympathy when action is needed, and the mailroom clerk who claims never to have received your request in the first place, are all wasting your time and theirs because they have not learned to say "No." To do this is simply poor ethics, poor business, poor personal relations, and it can make life harder for everyone in the future.

Compromises that Work

What can you do if the person doing the asking is your spouse, your boss, your child, your parent, or your best friend and you don't feel you can out-and-out say "No"? You can often satisfy other people and still not completely sacrifice your own priorities if you look for compromises.

When another person asks you to do something for him right away, he may well be more interested in speed than perfection. If you feel his demands on your time are reasonable, look for short-cuts. If your boss unexpectedly asks for a quick report on the month's sales, chances are he'll settle for a brief survey provided he gets it right away. If your daughter asks you on short notice to make her a new dress for a party, propose a quickly-made skirt instead.

Other people may habitually turn to you for particular tasks because you have, in effect, trained them to do so. Maybe it used to be your A to pack the family's lunches, but now that the kids are older, you've found an interesting selling job. You'll have to wean them away from having mother do it, perhaps by rotating the responsibility for preparing lunch. In business, you could encourage a demanding customer to go directly to the service department instead of depending on you for help, by explaining that his requests will be handled with greater speed.

Another solution to conflicting priorities (his A, your C) is discussion. If you feel harassed at home, try sitting down with your husband and listing your respective household duties. This will put into perspective how much you are already doing, and perhaps he'll see that all the demands on your time are unreasonable. This may never have occurred to him before, and you can adjust your duties to free more time for your A's.

When you are working in a cooperative effort with an associate, start by reviewing your To Do List and his. Look for those items which you both agree have high priority. Then try to enlarge the area of agreement by examining those items to which you have assigned different priorities. Express your point of view, and try to convince him that what he thought was an A is really a C. Listen to him, too, and try to understand his viewpoint. Be prepared to change your own assessment of the priorities if he can make a convincing case that what you called a C is really an A.

When agreement cannot be reached, trade-offs are a good idea. In return for doing his A (although it is of little value to you), ask that he do one of your A's. This also works well in reverse: "I won't ask you to do this if you don't ask me to do that" isn't childish; it can be a handy way to rid yourself of time-consuming C's by simple exchange.

Time-Sharing

When there are several people competing for your time and attention, some system that is fair to everyone generally works best. Sally of the steno pool, with half a dozen "bosses," does the work given to her in the order received. If Mr. Bracken has a special rush job, it gets immediate attention. If two people in the office need their work "right away," she can't satisfy both demands. But she can set her own priorities, point out the conflict and let them fight it out, or go to her supervisor for a decision.

Time-sharing, as fairness, can be particularly important to children, who will often compete for the time and attention of parents. For example, at our dinner table there is one seat—the one closest to my wife and me—that each of our children prefers. We'd like to have all our children sit next to us all the time but that's a physical impossibility. In the interest of fair play, we rotate the seat by using a simple numerical system, taking the day of the month and dividing it by three. If there's no remainder, it's our youngest child David's turn; if there's a remainder of one, our middle child Diane gets the seat; and if there's a remainder of two, the seat goes to Carol, the eldest.

At bedtime we use a different solution that assures each child an equal share of attention. Fortunately they go to bed at different times. My wife sets a timer, and just before bedtime, each child receives fifteen minutes of undivided parental attention to use in any way he or she wants.

Whichever of the many strategies you adopt to keep other

people's requests from swamping you, it pays to be gracious. And if you make a special effort to be considerate of other people and their time, they will be likely to respect you and your time.

And isn't that what you want—time to do your thing?

12. HOW TO CREATE QUIET TIME FOR YOURSELF

So YOU HAVE blocked out time on your calendar for heavy thinking. Now the question is: Will you be left alone so you can really concentrate? As any office worker knows, just because you decide you want to be alone doesn't mean that visitors and telephone calls will magically stop intruding. Furthermore, are you sure you really want everybody to stay away from you? Most people need to be in touch with other people to conduct their business. The point is that there are ways to regulate this traffic.

"Do you have a minute?" usually means "May I have your attention now to talk about something that will take an unspecified length of time?" So the next time someone asks, "Do you have a minute?" you might say, "Can we really do it in a minute?" or "Sure, I have a minute now, but if it takes longer we'll have to do it later."

Who is doing all the interrupting in the first place? Are they mostly V.U.P.'s (Very Unimportant Persons)? It pays to find out. The first thing to do, if interruptions are a problem, is keep a log of all telephone calls and visitors. Mr. Jackson, the director of a non-profit foundation, kept such a log for a week. It showed whether these time-snatchers were scheduled, who they were, and what they wanted. When he reviewed the log he found that the 80/20 rule applied. Eighty percent of his interruptions were coming from 20 percent of the interrupters. And by far most of the interruptions were coming from two people: an assistant and another subordinate.

This kind of traffic is easy to regulate, as I'll show you shortly. But even if your boss is in the habit of calling you into his office in the morning and wipes out your lovingly polished time plan by giving you an unexpected assignment that takes most of the day, you needn't commit harakiri. Try these ideas instead:

Encourage your boss to warn you about such tasks the day before, if at all possible, so that you may plan your time more realistically—not only for your benefit but for his. Is your boss (or client) giving unnecessary priority to tasks that could be adequately handled on a scheduled, non-rush basis, and might you point this out tactfully?

It's also worth asking yourself whether your boss is in the habit of turning to you for this type of assignment because you have in effect trained him to do so. If so, try being a bit less available, or delegate others to handle it instead. The same goes for a demanding customer. If the situation warrants, you may benefit from encouraging him to call the service department or some other person instead of always depending on you.

Mr. Jackson's case presented no great problem. He worked out a schedule with his assistant to see him at three scheduled times during the day: 9:30, 1:30, and 3:30. His assistant was to save all business for those times, except for the most urgent emergencies. The assistant had gotten into the habit of jumping up and rushing into Mr. Jackson's office like a fireman whenever anything came up. In the future he was never to interrupt Mr. Jackson unless convinced his mission was an A-item.

The other subordinate presented a different problem. This man, Anderson, was insecure in his job. In order to function, he needed continual reassurance that he was doing everything right. He was constantly bothering Mr. Jackson with a stream of low-priority (vague, but urgent-sounding) matters that he pressured Mr. Jackson to do right away. Also, Anderson was overdependent and unable to make a decision on his own. He insisted on droning through all the details even when Mr. Jackson didn't need them to make a choice.

On balance, though, Anderson had done good work, and Mr. Jackson had never wanted to hurt his feelings by telling him to stop bugging him with trivia. Now Mr. Jackson decided that Anderson's milquetoastish ways were a luxury he could no longer afford. Either Anderson would have to get along better on his own or he could be replaced by someone who didn't require so much of Mr. Jackson's time. Much as he liked Anderson, Jackson couldn't afford the time that he cost. Eventually Anderson was transferred to another department where he felt more secure, though the work was not as challenging.

The log kept by Mr. Frank, another executive, revealed a different pattern. Every two minutes or so he was interrupted by one of his many staff members. His solution was to reorganize, delegate more responsibility to his supervisors, and encourage his employees to look to the supervisors for answers to questions. He established weekly staff meetings, because his log revealed that several people were asking him for information requiring coordination with others. Mr. Frank also started sending background memos to the entire staff on routine matters, since lack of information was creating unnecessary interruptions of his work.

When the Interrupter is a Four-Year-Old

Ms. Jones didn't need a log to tell her that her day was being constantly interrupted by her four-year-old daughter, Melinda. When Ms. Jones wanted to find time to finish an exciting novel, she went into the bedroom, closed the door, and began reading. Within two minutes Melinda was on Mommy's lap. Disappointed, Ms. Jones consoled herself with the thought that Melinda would grow up better-adjusted for having had her mother's attention in her formative years, and went back to dreaming of next year, when Melinda would start a half day of kindergarten and Mommy would have all that time to herself.

Ms. Jones finally decided Melinda could be just as well-adjusted if she had her mother's wholehearted attention only some of the time instead of the half-hearted attention that is all any adult can muster when a child is watched without letup. After all, if Ms. Jones was in a better humor during her time with Melinda, she was sure to be a happier and more creative mother.

One day she got the courage to put a latch on the bedroom door, set the kitchen timer for thirty minutes, and told Melinda that she was going into her room to read for half an hour. She promised to play Fish when the timer bell went off. Melinda was to play in her room until it did.

You can't imagine the wailing and screams that Melinda produced from her side of the bedroom door, but Ms. Jones steeled herself and kept the door closed. She didn't get any reading done that first day because she was too anxious about the effect her experiment would have on Melinda, but she set the time for thirty minutes at 10:30 each day that week. By the end of the week Melinda seemed to have adjusted to the new system and played quietly in her room while Ms. Jones not only finished her novel but was halfway through a second one.

Contact Time vs. Thinking Time

If your log reveals that 80 percent of your interruptions are from new and/or different people, you obviously can't solve the problem by talking to the key interrupters. If your job involves a great deal of public contact, you'd best answer the phone or see the caller. But if you usually perform two roles, one requiring public contact and the other thinking alone, then you need some way to balance the demands of the two roles so that the contact role doesn't interrupt the thinking role to death.

Although he kept telling himself the new revision of his billing system was important, every time a visitor came his way Mr. Bean took time out to talk to him—even when it was a trivial matter that could have been handled by a subordinate.

Mr. Bean knew that the system revision was the big A-1, and he felt bad each evening when he went home after spending little time on it. He blamed the constant interruptions. The truth was that Mr. Bean blew hot and cold on interruptions. Sometimes he sought them out; at other times he resented even the important ones. When he was interrupted in the middle of an intricate part of the revision plan he was annoyed. Even if a very big customer was on the phone, Mr. Bean didn't think, "That's my job calling." Instead, he shrugged and fumed, "How can I get my work done?"

Mr. Bean's solution to the problem of conflicting job functions was to alternate between them, to the detriment of both. Was there a better way?

Mr. Bean contemplated not answering the phone and refusing to see visitors. This would give him time to think, and the system revision would probably get done nicely. But then what were the risks in not being available? He might offend other people who would want and expect to talk to him. His staff might fail to coordinate with him, and mix-ups might result. Morale might decline, because he might not learn of gripes and complaints until they had built to a crisis proportion.

What he did do was little better. He allowed anyone to see him any time. But rather than paying careful attention to their problems, he was often preoccupied with his own interrupted one. He was nervous and tense about getting back to his work," and since he was too "busy" to listen carefully, he made visitors sorry they had ever come.

Set Up Availability Hours

I suggested that perhaps a better solution would be to create special "Availability Hours." We're all familiar with signs saying: "Salesmen seen only Tuesday and Thursday from 1-4" or "The Doctor sees patients only on Monday, Tuesday and Wednesday." Availability Hours are those hours during the week when you're available to associates or others without appointment. At such times visitors may walk through your "open door" and feel free to discuss business, assured that their viewpoint will receive undivided attention. Mr. Bean decided to set up Availability Hours from 8 to 9:30 and again from 11 to 12 in the morning, leaving 9:30 to 11 as Quiet Time. He instructed the switchboard operator to take all routine calls during his Quiet Time so that he could work without interruption.

Quiet Time Can Backfire

Luckily, Mr. Bean remembered the case of Mr. Kent, who unexpectedly and unilaterally decreed that absolutely no one was to disturb him during Quiet Time between 8 and noon. The results were catastrophic. His subordinates struggled on their own, and hence made many more mistakes. Morale dropped, and his failure to take note of this reduced it even further. For a time Mr. Kent received congratulations from his boss. He seemed to be doing the right thing. The bravos died down when the state of organizational decline was fully appreciated. Eventually Mr. Kent was fired—in effect, because of his failure to balance Quiet Time and Availability Time.

So Mr. Bean discussed his proposed new arrangement with his key people and made changes based on their suggestions. Several thought they would try a little experimenting on their own, because they had also felt the need to get their own work done without interruptions. Mr. Bean made sure that they would bring to his attention any fallout that his proposed schedule might have on their jobs during the readjustment period.

How do you set aside Quiet Time and block out interruptions?

If you're a top executive, it's a cinch: just tell your secretary to take all your calls, turn any emergencies over to your Executive Assistant, and close the door of your private office.

If you don't have a secretary or switchboard operator to take your calls, you might tie up your telephone line a half hour a day by dialing your own number and leaving the phone off the hook so anyone calling you will get a busy signal.

You also need to keep others from coming by to talk to you during your Quiet Time.

Mr. Bean remained fair game for his colleagues so long as they saw that he was alone and therefore "not doing anything important." But then he told them about his idea of Quiet Time and put a sign on his desk that said "Quiet Time, please return at 11:30." Whenever someone approached him during Quiet Time, he pointed to the sign, asked whether the caller could wait until then, and made sure to get back to the interrupter promptly at 11:30.

When he was particularly in need of concentration, he looked around for an unused office or conference room. Sometimes he went to the public library. (A top executive confided to me that when he wanted Quiet Time he hid out in the back of a small coffee shop two blocks from his corporation's headquarters building.)

How To Handle the Sociables

Mr. Bean also found from his log that many people just stopped by to chat. He was on the main route to the water cooler and anyone running away from a difficult job back at his desk found him easy game for a few minutes of relaxing. He therefore shifted his desk to a different angle. Then he took away the extra visitor's chair, because he found that when two escapees got talking together at his desk it meant a minimum of twenty minutes' time wasted. Finally, he tried to keep his head down so that he didn't catch the eyes of passersby.

The next problem Mr. Bean encountered was that he became lonesome during Quiet Time. He was so accustomed to talking to people that he kept hoping someone would interrupt him. Every time the phone rang, even though he knew his secretary would pick it up, he couldn't help wondering who was calling and what they wanted. Although it took a lot of willpower, he resisted the tendencies to pick up the phone himself or to jump up right afterward to get the message.

He found it difficult not to be helpful to whomever came his way, and though his secretary managed to keep many visitors away, those in his own organization who ignored her and marched right into his office with "Do you have a minute?"-type questions usually got his attention.

Mr. Bean still found it difficult to say "no" to anyone. But when he tried it a few times, he was surprised: Nothing serious happened. He found that most of the interrupters were simply in the habit of coming in and really could wait until later—and so could his own need to have other people around. Gradually he became more firm. His tone indicated he was not angry with the interrupter, but he was insistent that the other person respect his Quiet Time.

Alternating Quiet Time with Availability Hours worked well for Mr. Bean and it can work well for you too.

13. ASK LAKEIN'S QUESTION

YOUR LIFETIME GOALS STATEMENT, your To Do List, and your Schedule give you substantial control over the way you spend your time. Each of these is an extremely valuable planning tool. But they are not handy for the minute-to-minute decisions you have to make.

Who can take fifteen minutes to plan a dozen times a day? Nobody. You wouldn't get anything done. Which is why I'm going to hand you a new tool to use quickly and spontaneously as many times a day as you need it. It's called "ask Lakein's Question." Lakein's Question is: *what is the best use of my time right now?*

At first you'll have to remind yourself to keep asking Lakein's Question whenever you're not positive whether you're using your time to best advantage. After a week or so it should become second nature to you.

If your first answer when you ask Lakein's Question is "I don't know," then the best use of your time is to ask the question again. If you still get "I don't know," then tell yourself: "I already know *that*; but I still need a better answer."

I don't mean to turn this into some silly game of hide-and-seek. I do suggest to you that if you really don't know the best use of your time, then there's nothing more important than finding out. So do keep asking Lakein's Question until you get at least some sort of meaningful answer.

As soon as you get the first answer, stop.

Almost invariably, the first (and spontaneous) answer to Lakein's Question is the best, and you should accept it. But a mistake *is* always a possibility. So take just a moment to make your "go/no-go" decision. Your intuition may have taken the morning off. If you feel you can't act on your first answer, it's best to come up with an acceptable alternative at once.

Like all new habits, asking Lakein's Question takes a bit of practice. As you adopt this routine, you'll find that your confidence increases, and that you come up consistently with good answers the first time around.

Ask Lakein's Question All the Time!

A particularly good time to ask Lakein's Question is when you have been interrupted by a visitor or telephone call (assuming that the interruption is desirable or necessary in the first place). When it's over, check whether you should go back to what you were doing or on to something new.

Also ask Lakein's Question when you notice that you are becoming distracted. Are you listening to a conversation in the next office? Wondering who just walked down the hall? Daydreaming about next year's vacation? Pop the question!

Also ask when you intuitively feel you may not be making the best use of your time. Or you detect a tendency to procrastinate. Or when you pause momentarily in the middle of doing an A-1. Or when you find yourself shuffling paper rather than processing it.

Ask it when you're torn between two different projects. When you run out of steam. Or at points where it seems natural to make the transition to something else.

To help you remember to ask Lakein's Question, put up signs around you saying "What is the best use of my time now?" and "Ask Lakein's Question" printed on them. The signs can be as visible as you wish. How about a large sign directly across from where you normally sit? How about using them as posters all over the house? Or if you want the signs to be less conspicuous, how about in a drawer or in your private notebook? You might even get some stationery with the question printed on it. (I once had pencils made up for my clients with Lakein's Question inscribed on them.)

Even if you know what the A-1 is and have started it, you can still ask Lakein's Question, but be a little more specific: What is the best use of my time now *on the A-1?* What part shall I do, and how shall I do it?"

Consider simplifying the task. Consider making it easier or faster. Should you phone or visit that slow-poke in the other department? Would it be better to write a letter to that long-winded customer so he doesn't gab on forever on the

phone—or do you really need a give-and-take discussion with
him to get a quick decision?

A fast work place is also a strength. The ability to work
very rapidly and perform well pays off, so check your work
pace periodically by asking Lakein's Question. Maybe you're
still hung up on last week's details. It happens.

You can also waste time on items that were once A's—but
are A's no longer. Is that big order likely to be canceled? Has
the deadline changed? Is that difficult account executive
about to get fired? A former A may decline in value to B and
then CZ not only with the passing of time, but also with the
degree of its completion. The 80/20 rule suggests that 80 percent of the value is often gained during the first 20 percent
of your work time on a certain task. Being a perfectionist
may mean that you're working much too hard to get only
minimum value.

When Perfectionism Helps—
and When It Doesn't

Perfectionism is worth approaching when 80 percent of the
value comes from the *last* 20 percent of the effort. For example: the construction of a dam, bringing home the family's
favorite groceries, unstopping a plugged-up sink, remembering your wedding anniversary every year.

Perfectionism is a waste of time on such labors as ironing
every last wrinkle out of a sheet or re-checking a low-priority letter for typing errors. Once you get immersed in some
activities, they seem to acquire a momentum of their own.
You may then be carried along without control, drifting with
the tide.

One way to combat this drift is to set yourself control
points for reviewing your progress. Check every fifteen minutes or half an hour—or go on until 3:30 and then review.
One way to remember to do this is to use a kitchen timer. If
you're not benefiting from continued effort, stop and change
to do something else.

You can also set the timer to help you meet deadlines. If
you need to get something done in half an hour, set the timer
accordingly. If you find the ticking annoying, put it in the
bottom drawer; then you'll hear only the bell. Suppose the
timer rings and you're still not finished? To protect yourself,

don't set the timer for thirty minutes; set it for twenty. Then you can re-set priorities after twenty minutes. Are you sure you're on the right track? You might want to set the timer for another fifteen minutes as a reminder that the project is probably not worth any more time.

Do you suspect diminishing returns? Are you being needlessly perfectionistic? Ask Lakein's Question. If you're not sure whether it is worth finishing something (or worth continuing), I suggest that you stop. If you don't come back to it, then in fact you were done. If you feel uncomfortable the next day about having stopped and you want to continue, go back to it. But pretty soon . . . right! Ask Lakein's Question again.

14. USING THE SWISS CHEESE METHOD

WHILE A CAREFULLY THOUGHT-OUT plan with well-defined goals and priorities is a giant step toward getting control of your time (and your life), even good planners often manage to forget one detail: A plan, like any tool, is valuable only if it's *used*. The best plans remain daydreams until you bring them to life through action.

In the case of most routine tasks—such as eating or brushing your teeth—planning leads directly to action. Even when you tackle more complex activities, planning and doing may be so closely tied together that they seem parts of the same step. A good plan—a plan that in all ways *feels* right to you—has a way of getting you to act on it simply because it's in front of you. After you finish such a plan, it draws you right into starting on the high-priority items.

At other times this transition from planning to action goes less smoothly. Let's assume that as a result of your planning (Listing/Setting Priorities, answering Lakein's Question) you've zeroed in on a particular task as your A-1: Today you're going to wash all the windows in the house! But instead of acting on your plan, you hesitate. Perhaps you feel like turning to a less-important task, or quitting for the day to go to a movie or merely to draw doodles in the dirt on the windows. Your attitude toward doing the A-1 is "do it later" rather than "do it now." Perhaps, for reasons I've discussed earlier (see Chapter 10), you'll settle on doing a C-task.

I've talked with thousands of people about their efforts to gain control of their time and their lives. Again and again I hear the familiar refrain, "For years I've been wanting to do this, but I keep putting it off," or "I know just what to do but I can't find time to get started."

Procrastination! It's one of the major stumbling blocks everybody faces in trying to achieve both short-term and long-term goals. But rather than let procrastination seize control of you, how about doing something positive?

Have You Picked the Correct A-1?

When you've identified an A-1 but find yourself reluctant to "do it now," take a fresh look at your choice. Your reluctance may be based on an intuitive feeling that the A-1 is not, after all, the best use of your time. Your intuition is often right. Avoiding the A-1 may be a smarter decision than your selection of the A-1 in the first place. Suppose your A-1 is learning how to sail, but you find that the instructor charges more than you can afford. Not following through on your plan may be the wisest course.

Perhaps your choice of an A-1 was the right one at the time, but now your priorities have suddenly and unexpectedly shifted. You have to forego spring housecleaning this week because Aunt Mary from Boston arrives on your doorstep three days early for her annual visit. Or you sit down at your desk to pay some bills when the mailman delivers a letter from your bank saying your last check bounced. Obviously, your A-1 is to straighten out your messed-up checking account; paying the bills will have to wait.

Putting off work on an A-1 is also wise when you find it will lead to consequences you didn't foresee when you sat down to plan. An advertising executive had decided that the best use of his time would be to respond to a big manufacturer's request for a preliminary presentation of an advertising campaign that might bring the advertising man a lot of additional business. He was disturbed because he had failed to follow through on this request for several weeks.

After brooding about this failure, he finally realized what was holding him back. Although this was an account he had long wanted, he knew that if he landed it, he would spend the next several months designing a huge campaign from scratch. But he already felt terribly overworked as it was. No wonder he was reluctant to tackle his A-1!

Once the advertising executive realized this, he knew that his problem was not procrastination but a matter of priorities. His real A-1 should have been to do something to ease (rather than add to) his work pressures, so he spent the next week training a subordinate to take over some of his routine work. Only then did he go back to thinking about the new account. He started in immediately, and, no longer held back by his former reluctance, he created a stunning proposal that landed the account.

So if you don't follow through on a plan because the choice is not current or valid, your delay is not due to procrastination, but to a desire to be flexible and adaptable. You're right not to go forward with your first A-1. The best course is to downgrade the former A-1. Pick out a new A-1 that better fits your changed priorities or unexpected opportunities, and make sure you "do it now."

Procrastination is . . .

Procrastination is when you've come up with a good A-1 activity, validated your choice, and found at least some minutes you could have spent on that A-1, and you are still not with it. Instead, you are doing a lesser A, a B, a C, or maybe even a task that you should admit is not worth doing at all. What in the world is wrong with you?

Mostly, you're just being human. And like most of my clients you undoubtedly procrastinate most on "Overwhelming A-1s" and "Unpleasant A-1s." People put off doing an Overwhelming A-1 because it seems too complex or too time-consuming (such as washing all the windows, redecorating the house, cataloging the slides of your last six years' vacations, mastering Russian, preparing your tax return when you claim a lot of deductions, moving to a new house, selling your business to retire, planning a trip around the world).

An Unpleasant A-1, on the other hand, is manageable, all right, but you're eager to avoid it because of some odious association, which is usually emotional (disciplining an employee, admitting an awkward mistake to your boss, telling your boss *he* made a mistake, presenting your husband with the bill for a very expensive dress).

These two categories are not mutually exclusive. Anybody can think of activities that seem both overwhelming and unpleasant. Still, the distinction remains useful in part because the strategies for dealing with each are different. The next several chapters will be devoted to a discussion of how to handle the problem of procrastination on an Overwhelming A-1. After that I will turn to ways to stop procrastinating on the Unpleasant A-1.

CAUTION: All the techniques to stop procrastinating are to be used only when genuinely necessary. It would be a great waste of your time to keep working with these techniques rather than doing your A-1. The goal, as ever, is to *select your A-1* and *do it now*. The techniques are simply means to an end and that end is to make better use of your time.

How to Overwhelm the Overwhelming A-1

Suppose you're at home and have just finished some chores. Your son will return from school in half an hour. You'd like to start on a painting you've been thinking about for weeks, but you wash up a few dirty dishes and mop the kitchen floor instead. After all, how can you possibly accomplish anything on your painting when you know you'll be interrupted so soon?

Or suppose you're at work and you've just finished a phone call. As you put down the receiver, you think to yourself that the best use of your time right now—the A-1—is to start work on the time-consuming, complex task of preparing the annual budget for your department. You glance at your watch. It's ten minutes before you usually go to lunch. A stack of routine paperwork is sitting on one corner of your desk, awaiting your attention. What should you do? Get a couple of quick paperwork C's out of the way? Or put ten minutes into the A-1-task, even though you feel quite overwhelmed by the prospect? Or go to lunch early?

The best answer—which is to get started on that Overwhelming A-1 even with only a few minutes at your disposal—seem unrealistic, even meaningless. You may well decide to get a few easy C's out of the way instead. On the face of it, this does not seem to be a very serious breach of good time-management practices, except that a person's day is typically divided up into bits and pieces. Let's face it: Large blocks of uninterrupted time are a comparative rarity. If again and again—a few minutes before lunch or before your child returns from school—you choose to work on the easy C

rather than to begin the difficult A-1, then you are procrastinating; you're avoiding what is really important.

In most cases, when a person turns to the short and easy
C, he does so precisely because it *is* short and easy. What you
need is some way to make the Overwhelming A-1 competitive with the easy C.

But how? Let's say you have estimated that it'll take you
fifty hours to formulate the budget, and you have only those
ten minutes available before lunch. The fact that you cannot
find anything like fifty hours today may well cause you to put
off starting the project until tomorrow. But of course there
aren't fifty hours available the next day either, so you may
delay day after day until, with the deadline looming, you finally make a frantic effort to get the job done—and probably
none too well, because you're in such a rush.

The key to getting an Overwhelming A-1 under control is
to get started on it as soon as you've identified it as the A-1
task. And an excellent way to get moving is to turn such an
Overwhelming A-1 into "Swiss Cheese" by poking some holes
in it. I call these holes "instant tasks."

An instant task requires five minutes or less of your time
and makes some sort of hole in your Overwhelming A-1. So
in ten minutes before lunch you have time for two instant
tasks. To find out what the first two should be, (1) make a
list of possible instant tasks, and (2) set priorities.

Here are some Swiss Cheese moves toward tackling the
budget problem: getting a copy of last year's budget, deciding on the people you'll need to contact, obtaining the files
you'll need, arranging a meeting to discuss the budget, or
going to lunch with a subordinate and turning over part of
the task (or all the preliminaries) to him. The only rule for
making up your list of possible instant tasks is to limit it to
items that can be started quickly and easily and are in some
way connected with working on the Overwhelming A-1.

What Five Minutes Can Do

The underlying assumption of the Swiss Cheese approach is
that it is indeed possible to get something started in five minutes or less. And once you've started, you've given yourself
the opportunity to keep going. For example, you may become so interested in reading one of the files that you study

it for forty-five minutes before realizing how hungry you are. Swiss Cheese may well become your lunch—non-fattening but eminently satisfying.

It's just as likely that you will start somewhere only to find that it quickly leads to a dead end. You try to call someone to arrange a meeting on the budget for after lunch. He's not available until tomorrow. So now you feel satisfied that you've done your bit on *that* project for the day. You may even be glad to have failed in your first effort; it's such a convenient excuse for further procrastination! That's an unpromising start. Swiss Cheese is supposed to lead to *involvement*.

So if that first effort failed, be patient for another moment. Think of a new instant task and give it a try.

Don't try to bite the same hole out of the cheese twice. If you've tried an instant task and it didn't lead to involvement, the next step is to try another instant task right away. And remember: One hole does not make a piece of Swiss Cheese. It may take a number of instant tasks before you finally get involved with the big A-1 and gather the momentum needed to stay with it.

One nice thing about the Swiss Cheese method is that it doesn't really matter what instant task you select as long as it's (1) easy—the easier the better—and (2) related to the Overwhelming A-1. How much of a contribution a particular instant task will make to getting your A-1 done is far less important than the overriding objective of the moment: To do something—anything—on the A-1. Whatever you choose, you'll at least have begun.

The Swiss Cheese approach sometimes makes it possible to achieve surprising inroads even on a complex project. After you've made ten or twelve holes in an Overwhelming A-1, you may discover with delight that the task turns out to be much less difficult than you'd expected. Perhaps you've found a way to turn over much of the project to someone else. Or you've discovered an unsuspected short cut. Or the job turns out to be easy and fun. Maybe all that was required was to break up the task into manageable bites; after you've done this some jobs, like some jigsaw puzzles, are easily completed.

Make A Last-Ditch Try

If you can't bring yourself to tackle the A-1, perhaps you should compromise. Suppose you've managed so far today to escape from the A-1. Before you go on to other things, make one last-ditch try at getting involved. Look at your watch and note the time. Spend exactly five minutes on the A-1 and then stop for the day. Surely you can stand almost any task for five minutes!

Picture yourself on your summer vacation by the lake. You've been lingering on the shore imagining how cold the water must be. You ask some people standing at the water's edge, and they tell you that it's really cold. They've gone in, though, and seem to have enjoyed it. You'd like to try it, too, but you're leery of the cold water.

Finally, you walk to the end of the dock and put your big toe into the water—it feels cold, all right. You put your whole foot in—it feels colder. You sit down and painfully put both feet into the water—it's colder still. You let your knees relax, and the water comes up to your calves—it's painfully cold.

This bit-by-bit torture is getting you down, so you tell yourself you'll quit in five minutes. You stand up. Should you jump or dive in? You decide to jump in, swim the fifty feet to the float, swim back, and—if you aren't enjoying it by then—climb out, dry yourself off, and play Ping-Pong.

There doesn't seem to be any right time to jump in. You decide to count down from one hundred. One hundred, ninety-nine, ninety-eight, . . . each number comes slower than the one before it. Four, three, two, one, jump! You're in the water and swimming toward the float.

Go Ahead: Quit If You Must

An hour later you may still be in the water—if you decided you liked the exuberance of swimming and playing in the chilly water. If you quit after five minutes you'll be waiting your turn for a rematch with the Ping-Pong king.

Back home the following week, you might wonder whether you can use this "quit in five minutes" guarantee to start exercising. Your doctor said you need more exercise.

You've already bought the exercise manual, but the exercises look too awful for words. Each morning during the two weeks before your vacation you got out of bed and groaned, "No, not today. Maybe tomorrow."

You're tired of groaning and would like to be in better shape. You decide that surely you can take five minutes of exercise. You get the kitchen timer and set it for five minutes. You open the manual and begin the exercises, keeping one eye on the clock. As soon as it rings, you're saved by the bell from further exertion and you groan in relief. You haven't given up groaning, but at least you've begun your exercise regime. Maybe the same trick will work again tomorrow. Maybe you might gradually increase the time to six, seven, or possibly eight minutes.

Back at work you find that you can use this "quit in five minutes" teaser to get yourself involved. You realize that you are delaying the A-1 project because you fear the worst, but once you get into it things will not be as awful as you imagine them to be (isn't that often the case?). So you spend five minutes and do a little experimenting. You dip gingerly into some aspect of the A-1.

What did you learn? Was the A-1 as unpleasant as you imagined? Was it dull? Was it really all that overwhelming? Was it that diifficult? Will it take that many hours? Isn't there any hope of success?

You can't expect to get too good an answer to all these questions in just five minutes. And if you happen to forget about them as your interest in the A-1 increases, it really doesn't matter. If this effort did not get you off and running on the A-1, at least you know a little more than you did before. Maybe your subconscious will help you come up with a fresh approach to the A-1 tomorrow. And don't try to tell yourself that you would have spent all Wednesday afternoon working on the A-1 if you hadn't spent five minutes today and discovered how unpleasant it is! You know deep down inside that the first five minutes Wednesday would have been your quota for the day. Now you can spend your *second* five minutes on it Wednesday—or perhaps the whole afternoon.

At other times you'll find, even after ten or twenty instant tasks, that you still have a complex and time-consuming project ahead of you. You are unlikely to finish a twelve-hour job by working only in five-minute bites. You'll have to set aside large blocks of time, hours or days, to complete it. I suggest you take your calendar and lay out a schedule of an hour a day, except for three hours each Tuesday and Thursday afternoon (or whatever) until the twelve hours have been reserved. Then let the logic of the task itself dictate steps to keep it moving.

The instant tasks may not have gotten the project finished, but they have led you to explore various aspects of it. You have become involved in an interesting question here, a challenging problem there. The project begins to exert a stronger and stronger pull. You become more eager to get back to it. You've zeroed in on your target. You're involved; you no longer need the crutch of instant tasks. You have stopped procrastinating. You're doing the A-1!

The method, I think you'll agree, sounds good. On the following pages I'll describe a wide range of instant tasks—quick, easy ways to get started—that will not only aid in eliminating procrastination, but will help break up any large task into smaller, more do-able activities.

15. HOW TO FIND INSTANT TASKS FOR INSTANT INVOLVEMENT

Do More Detailed Planning

So YOU'RE HAVING TROUBLE getting involved in the A-1. Are you sure you've really drawn a bead on exactly what it is you want to accomplish? If that's your trouble, you probably need to do more detailed planning. As a general rule, the more detailed the plan, the better the chance that action will follow. And remember: Planning is really decision-making.

First, I'm going to show you how to make some decisions to solidify your feelings about the A-1.

Take a piece of paper and head it "I have decided." You are now ready for five minutes of Decision Time.

Record on the paper whatever decisions come to your mind about the A-1. For instance: when to start it; what to do first; what to do next; how much time you can devote to it all together; what information you need; what equipment is required; who else will be involved. The more concrete decisions you can make, the more likely it is you'll fix on some simple but valuable ways to start on the A-1 and get involved.

If you run into snags doing this kind of detailed planning, I recommend you try "The Magic If."

Admit to yourself: "I just cannot plan." Then say to yourself, "But if I *could* plan, what would the plan be?" Now, set about to answer the *if* question. The beauty of the "I can't . . . but if I could . . . question is that it temporarily frees you from all the limitations and problems you face. It unblocks the planning muscles, as many of my clients have discovered.

Or imagine this: You've been relieved of all responsibility for getting a difficult A-1 done. Instead, you only have to write down a plan for someone else to follow. You're simply to give this person whatever good advice you can, based on your familiarity with the project up to now. Once you've prepared your plan, the entire burden of carrying out the plan will be shifted to his shoulders. You never have to *do* anything. Your only task is to plan how someone else should do it.

Now, what would you recommend to this person? Don't worry if some of the steps you recommend might be difficult for you. The other fellow will be the one to do them—that is what he's there for.

Next, put the written plan in the center of your desk and take a break. Go to the water cooler. Talk with a friend. Relax. When you return to your desk, look at the written plan the other person is going to follow and see if there is anything you might do to help him out. You will probably find there are steps within the plan involving work that you're particularly good at or that you enjoy doing. Until the other fellow shows up, how about getting going on these preferred parts of the plan, just to start the A-1 rolling?

It's a fact: not only can The Magic If make it possible for you to plan what is to be done, it will often enable you to follow through as well.

Get More Information

Sometimes I just can't get started on a project no matter how hard I try. I once decided to lay a patio in my backyard. But I knew nothing about the materials or tools I was going to need. I never did start working on my patio.

This is a common chain, and a deadly one. You don't have the information. You don't get really interested. You can't become involved. No action.

The old adage about familiarity breeding contempt is often untrue. Non-familiarity often leads to lack of interest. I once read of an experiment with high school students who were presented with a list of forty-eight questions about invertebrate animals. The students were asked to indicate the twelve questions to which they would most like to know the answers. Surprise! Questions about familiar animals were picked more often than questions about unfamiliar animals.

In another study, students were shown some unusual objects borrowed from museums. The experimenter went through the collection of objects three times, giving more information each time around. Whenever an object was presented, the students were asked to indicate on a 1-to-5 scale the extent to which they wanted to know more about it. There was a significant tendency for more curiosity to be expressed with each successive appearance of an object.

Here is experimental evidence that it takes at least a little information to generate an interest in something. The same is true in our everyday experience. Listener surveys of radio and TV news programs show that people who listen to the six-o'clock news often listen to the 11 o'clock news as well. The same people who listen to the news regularly are likely to read one or two newspapers seriously. Some information leads to eagerness for more.

Who reads hobby magazines? People who already know something about the hobby. Whether it's model railroading, skiing, or gardening, most readers of such publications are regular readers eager for new ideas. Someone just glancing at such magazines on a newsstand may well wonder how anyone could find them interesting. Lacking background knowledge and a frame of reference, they find the details meaningless.

Not until a certain level of familiarity with a subject is reached are people likely to push toward a further exploration to satisfy the newly aroused curiosity. Once that level is reached, there is a good chance that involvement will increase as knowledge accumulates—which is why getting more information is an instant task that leads to involvement.

Reading is one of the easiest instant tasks for most people. Looking at books, magazines, newspapers, internal reports, memoirs, files, or letters for even a few minutes may stimulate your interest in a subject that you never much cared about before—and it's leisurely activity that requires little energy.

Another good way to get more information is to talk to people. People in your organization. In your neighborhood. In your family. Talking is a pleasant way to get more information about your A-1.

Try a Leading Task

When you really aren't quite up to doing anything on your A-1, but are not averse to getting ready to do something, taking a physical step can often be a way of easing yourself gradually into the big job. I call this a "leading task" because it leads you on.

An obvious instant task to get you started on writing a report is to make some notes on the points to be covered. But suppose even this seems too much to tackle. Try sharpening a pencil. I'm not joking! Involvement will not necessarily ensue, but at least there is a chance that, once you have the freshly sharpened pencil in your hand, you will let the pencil impel you to write a few words of value before you put it down again.

The physical presence of some item associated with your A-1 can also be a compelling stimulus leading to involvement. A good leading task is to move such an item to a conspicuous place. You have a letter that you know you should answer, but have been avoiding. Try putting it right in the middle of your desk. This increases the chance that sooner or later you will pick it up and get started on a reply, perhaps when you are seeking diversion from some other task. Another good leading task is to remove all distractions from your desktop (such as expense accounts, cocktail-party invitations, or that copy of *Playboy*). Your chances that you will turn to the A-1 will materially increase if it's the only item staring you in the face.

If you really want to read *War and Peace*, but just don't seem to get around to it, here are some good leading tasks. Buy a copy. Take it off your bookshelf. Put it in your favorite reading chair. Leave it lying around opened to page 1. Show it to a friend and say, "I've finally started on this!"

People often tell me about some hobby they once enjoyed but now only dream about. One man told me how much he regretted that he hadn't played tennis in five years. I learned that his tennis racket was at the bottom of a storage chest, and that the only tennis balls he owned were old and had no bounce. No wonder playing tennis was just a dream for him!

Doing a leading task would certainly increase this man's

chances of once again enjoying a game of tennis. He might have his racket restrung. Or buy some new tennis balls. Or put all his equipment in the trunk of his car. If he still found himself driving past an empty tennis court without stopping, he could put his racket on the front seat so that he had to move it to get into his car. With this constant stimulus—or irritant—as a reminder, if he's really serious about wanting to play tennis, he'll eventually take his racket out of his car, and even hit a few balls. Whether he'll remain involved is another matter—which we shall turn to later. In any case, he will have gotten started and at least given himself the chance to continue.

One of my clients decided to wake up a little earlier each morning to find time for a new interest. Setting his alarm ahead half an hour did no good because he went right back to sleep. I suggested he try a leading task. He moved the alarm clock from beside his bed to the other side of his room, right in front of the bathroom door. Getting up to turn off the alarm put him very close to the bathroom, so it required only a bit more effort to go to the sink and brush his teeth. Having brushed his teeth, he was free to go back to sleep. He found, however, that if he could just manage to brush his teeth, he was up to stay, because for years and years he had made it a practice never to go back to bed after brushing his teeth!

Many of the most effective leading tasks take only a moment or two. We all know that there is often a very definite connection between clenching one's jaw and being determined; between leaning forward in a chair and being alert; between taking a deep breath and relaxing. When you act to place yourself within these patterns you can lead yourself on in the direction you want to go. Many of us do this without even thinking about it. If you look directly at a speaker, you're more likely to listen to him. If you stand up and stretch during an evening's reading, you are less likely to fall asleep. Consciously look for opportunities to use these kinds of physical actions to help you do what you want, and you'll find them.

Still another useful leading task is to "select the right channel." That is: If you have nothing to say, at least turn your mind toward the outlet that you'd use if you were full of ideas. If you must type something, turn on the typewriter.

Title a page something like "I can't think of anything to type." Then pour out your soul to the typewriter—type anything that goes through your mind, anything at all. After doing this for a while, your mind may be jogged so you're ready to put a fresh piece of paper in the typewriter and start typing something connected with the A-1.

If you need to dictate, turn on your dictation machine and *keep it on* even if you don't have anything to say. Gradually, the running dictation belt may start to pull you along, almost forcing you to find something to say. Once the words have begun to flow, you can direct them toward the A-1. If you do not turn on your dictation machine until you have precisely the "right thing" to say, you may never get started.

If you are having trouble making an important telephone call, pick up the phone and call a friend. Try to explain to your friend that it's impossible for you to pick up the phone, dial the numbers, say hello, and talk to this other person. But wait! You've just done it. If you can do it once, you can do it again and make that A-1 call.

Leading yourself toward the A-1 in this way will not always work. But I have observed many times that a simple physical action does indeed lead to meaningful involvement.

Take Advantage of Your Current Mood

One reason why people have difficulty getting involved in their A-1 is that it often requires doing something they're not emotionally prepared to do. Perhaps getting started on your A-1 means sitting quietly at your desk thinking, when what you really feel like doing is talking to someone. Now you have two options: To forget all about your decision to get started on the A-1 and talk to someone just for the sake of talking, or to take advantage of your mood by letting it carry you toward the A-1, rather than away from it.

The idea is to take your emotional need and see whether it is possible to satisfy it in some way connected with the A-1. In the example I just gave, clearly the best use of your time would be to go to talk to someone who is concerned with your A-1 and see what ideas he or she can share with you. After satisfying your need for companionship, and hopefully getting some good ideas in the bargain, you may find it much easier to return to your desk and do the required thinking.

The reverse twist of this—leading to procrastination rather than forward movement—happens daily in most stockbrokerage offices. Many people become stockbrokers in part because of a wish to associate with (and help) other people. Rationally, this could be satisfied by calling on prospects and customers and attempting to sell stocks. This need can also be satisfied by talking to other stockbrokers. Besides, stockbrokers are handier, and known for their friendliness; prospects are more difficult to reach, and occasionally of less friendly bent.

That is why many stockbrokers use up much valuable time by selling other brokers on their views about sports, politics and women.

At times everybody likes to be left alone to shuffle papers quietly. This is a legitimate emotional need, often satisfied by processing routine paperwork, emptying the in-box, or neatening a pile of more or less useless memos. If you detect that you're avoiding your A-1 because of this need, you may be able to satisfy it and still do something for the A-1. You could arrange all your papers connected with the A-1 in alphabetical order, dot all the i's and cross all the t's, make neat lists of things to do on the A-1 (without any feeling of ever having to do them), or rewrite a memo about the A-1 even though the memo really needs no further polishing.

You might well ask me at this point, "Aren't I better off doing something worthwhile that is not connected with the A-1 rather than doing something trivial on the A-1?"

My emphatic answer to this question is "No!"

If you tell me you've been procrastinating and are not able to get involved in the A-1, do anything, regardless of importance, so long as it has *some* connection with the A-1. Once you're involved, your sense of priorities will lead you eventually to do more productive work on the A-1. But if you turn to some other activity, you've done nothing to try to halt the procrastination mechanism, and you've given yourself no chance to become involved.

Sometimes it's best to wait until your mood is right for doing something. You don't want to use up too much energy trying to force yourself to do something that you don't want to do. But often—especially if the task you have identified as your A-1 is fairly complex and involves a number of steps—there is an excellent chance that at least one particular aspect of the project will fit your current mood. Your job is to find that soft spot.

A good question to ask yourself at this point is "What am I *willing* to do on the A-1?" You might say to yourself, "I know there are plenty of things about this A-1 that I don't feel like doing now, but is there *anything* I find interesting, or appealing, or at least tolerable?"

Find some piece of the A-1 that you're in the mood to do. Then you will be using your existing needs to lead you toward the A-1 rather than letting them lead you away from it.

Say you're writing a book. At this moment you're not interested in rewriting any of the dozen chapters that will have to be completely reworked. You *do* feel like reading the editor's comments on those chapters that are in pretty good shape, and that require little effort on your part to finish up.

Or you face a big exam. You're not quite ready to read the supplementary textbooks that the professor has assigned. But you don't mind reading over your class notes, something you know you're going to have to do anyway in the course of preparing for the test.

Give Yourself a Pep Talk

Perhaps your lack of involvement is due to a lack of motivation. In that case, taking a few minutes to build up motivation is a good investment.

Studies have shown that most people don't start a project they believe they can't finish. Conversely, most people will attempt something that appears easy even though in fact it is impossible. The basis of their willingness to try is their subjective estimate of the probability of success.

So remember: If you *feel* that something will be difficult or impossible, the odds are that you'll not be as likely to try it as if you feel it is easy. But keep in mind that these are your feelings. They aren't necessarily facts. Since you don't for a fact know how hard something is, you'll do better to assume that it's not too difficult and that you can do it. This is much more likely to get you started on the A-1. It stands to reason: If you think you're going to be successful, you'll work harder on getting the A-1 finished—which is why a little pep talk about positive attitude and self-confidence can motivate you to do the A-1. Just as the coach talks to the football team at halftime, you might try telling yourself:

"You can do it. So stay with it."

"Stop feeling sorry for yourself and get to work!"

"You'll never know until you try."

"We don't want any defeatists around here."

These slogans will help fight discouragement and negative feelings.

Your pep talk might also include a listing of the benefits (see Learn to Stress the Benefits, Chapter 20) that you'll reap from getting the A-1 done, and yes, the consequences that face you if you fail to do it now. (See The Real Price Of Delay, Chapter 19).

Make a Commitment to Someone

You tell yourself, "I'll spend an hour on this in the afternoon," but the time comes and goes and you work on other matters. But if you have actually made an appointment with someone else to discuss the subject, you're likely to keep the appointment and get the subject discussed, because you've made a commitment to someone and don't want to let that person down. I find that some clients use an appointment with me as the stimulus to get going on some A-1 they feel is important. They don't want to let me down, and they don't want to waste the fee they're paying me. They've made a commitment in self-esteem and money, and these are powerful stimuli indeed.

What can you promise, and who is a good promisee? Well, you can promise your husband to get the garden in shape in time for the backyard barbeque he has arranged; promise your wife, as she leaves for the office in the morning, that you'll make a soufflé for dinner tonight; promise your boss that you'll have the proposal ready for his review on his return from his Toledo trip. Usually this kind of promise activates your conscience sufficiently to get the A-1 done.

A deadline, though often unpleasant, also seems to force action. A promise to meet a deadline rather than do it "later" is a good inducement. If friends invite you to "get together sometime" you may well want to leave things deliberately vague. But if you really enjoy their company, don't let them get away without setting a definite time for getting together.

A meeting is a special kind of deadline. A commitment to be a particular place at a specific time to discuss a particular subject goes a long way to get a task moving. Your unwillingness to be totally unprepared at the meeting forces your hand. You do some preparation, and this represents more involvement than you've mustered up to now.

Meetings are one of the greatest time-wasters ever invented. They are almost always inefficient. Much of what is said at meetings is irrelevant or redundant. Little is to the point. But what do you expect? If the guy who called the meeting knew all the answers, or could just go ahead and do what needed doing, he wouldn't have called the meeting in the first place.

Most meetings come about because someone cannot do the A-1 easily or by himself. Rather than leaving important problems totally unattended to, the executive committee of the Supergiant Corporation of the membership committee of the YMCA gets everyone together and at least gets someone thinking about the A-1 problem. It might be an instant task to call a meeting, but it's hardly an instant task to attend it. As I've shown, you can usually do a lot better yourself.

16. TRY STIMULUS CHANGE TO KEEP INVOLVED

ONCE YOU GET INVOLVED, many tasks keep you involved until the end. You may put off cleaning up after a dinner party for several hours, but once you *do* begin—washing the dishes, cleaning the ashtrays, vacuuming the rug—you persevere until the job is done. Or, having put aside a couple of hours of quiet time, you spread across your desk all the hotel, airline, and rent-a-car receipts from a long business trip and keep at it until you have filled out all the necessary expense account forms so your office will reimburse you.

Most tasks are sufficiently short or compelling so that even if you must put them aside and come back to them later, your initial involvement carries you quickly back to the heart of the project, just as a good book pulls at you again and again until you have read the last page.

At other times you work on a task for a while, but you run out of steam short of your goal. Perhaps you've been sitting at your desk working on the proposal for a new television documentary for an hour and a half, and can't come up with another decent idea. Or you've been addressing envelopes for a charity benefit; you have to finish by 5 P.M. but halfway through you just can't stand to look at another zip code.

You know that the best use of your time is to continue with the A-1. You have told yourself that this is no time for procrastination. You managed to get involved. You built up quite a bit of momentum. But now you're bogged down. How you can possibly stay involved any longer?

One answer is: Always set a next step. Quite frequently, a project will bog down for lack of planning the very next step. Whenever you are working your way through a project, make clear what the next step is. Then set a time to check whether you've completed that step.

119

No Need to Become Bored

It's not at all surprising that you should become bored, restless, or fatigued after working on the same task for some time. The yearning for change is natural. Variety is not merely "the spice of life"; it's an essential ingredient.

Various experiments have been carried out in which an individual is placed in a room with a strictly controlled environment. His responses are monitored. In one of these experiments the subject lies on a comfortable bed in total darkness most of the time. All his physical needs are cared for. He pushes a button and finds a hot meal behind a sliding panel. After five days of this, most of the test subjects reported hysteria, fantasies, and delusions. No subject was able to continue for more than a week, and all took many months to recuperate fully. Such experiments confirm that in the absence of what is called "stimulus change" a person undergoes rapid psychological deterioration.

If stimulus change is a fundamental human need, this need may go back to the way our ancestors lived. The caveman's life depended on his ability to detect and respond to change. A shift in the scent carried on the wind alerted him to the presence of food and the danger of predatory animals. Survival of the fittest favored those who were most sensitive to stimulus change. Modern man has inherited this biological radar.

But if it once was a matter of life and death to be aware of a sound of the advancing mammoth's footsteps, today it is generally annoying and distracting to be turned into the noise of strangers walking down the hall, other people's telephones ringing, and cars passing by.

Potentially distracting stimuli are always around although when you're very much engrossed in something, you may not notice them or can ignore them. Constructive stimuli sometimes need an invitation.

Normally your need for stimulus change is satisfied by the evolution of the current task as one step leads to another. The natural evolution of a project generates many possible tasks. Keeping a To Do List gives you a choice of tasks to provide stimulus change. It even pays occasionally to take time to list additional steps you might take on the A-1 just so you have a broader range of activities to draw upon.

It's when the current task does not provide variety and change of pace that you grow restless or bored and eagerly accept distraction or create it for yourself. Is there any alternative to procrastination at this point?

Suppressing your need for change is very unlikely to be a satisfactory way of staying involved in the A-1 when you feel like you've had enough; you can't change the biologically instilled need for stimulus change. If you're going to get control of your actions, your opportunity comes in providing the *right* stimulus change.

Rest Breaks and Work Breaks

One thing you can do is take a rest break. Get up and stretch, walk to the water cooler, socialize, then continue on the A-1 for another hour or two.

You can also take a work break. Any other task will do, but another A is always preferable if it will mean a change of pace from the work you were just involved in. If you've been addressing envelopes, make an appointment with your hairdresser, go over your dinner menu, wash the breakfast dishes, or visit with the woman next door. Then, after a few minutes, go back and continue the A-1.

Often the break is all you need. But what do you do if you're working against a deadline and every minute counts? Or if you tried a coffee break ten minutes ago and you're already becoming restive again? You might leave the A-1 for a while, but is that wise? Won't you have the same problem of reinvolvement when you try to return to it later?

You really want to stick to it, but how?

The answer lies in satisfying your need for stimulus change *within* the scope of the A-1.

Tasks that you find dull and repetitive can—with some imagination—be made more interesting. Even if you're sending out Christmas cards, sewing name tapes on camp clothes, or coding inventory sheets, if you look you will find ways to vary such tasks and satisfy your need for stimulus change without running away to some other activity.

The real payoff in using this technique comes when you're

having trouble staying involved in a multifaceted project, like writing a magazine article, developing a study proposal for the League of Women Voters, figuring out how to respond to a competitor's new product, or researching ways to recycle used plasterboard. To keep from procrastinating when you get bogged down in a swampy part of the forest, you need to get hooked on some new aspect of the project. You need fresh bait for fresh involvement.

As I showed in the section on instant tasks, there are many ways to move your project ahead. You can plan, talk to others, give yourself a pep talk, gather information, write down some notes. Naturally, some projects have more built-in variety than others. But there are always at least *some* opportunities for change within each project.

Try changing your location. Sometimes new surroundings can do wonders to refresh a tired mind. If you've been working at your desk, try the conference room. If you've been reading in the living room, try the bedroom. Or stay where you are but change your position. If you have been sitting down, try standing on your head.

What works best is to change the way you're going about the task. Any intellectual effort contains elements that can be juggled. You need information and ideas. These have to be collected, digested, and acted upon. You can shift back and forth between working on information and ideas, or switch from collecting to digesting to action.

Not Enough Information—or Too Much?

Let's begin with information collection. Earlier I discussed the idea of getting more information as a way to get involved. You will recall that the level of your interest generally increases as you move from no information to some information. So when you need to keep involved in a project, pick an area where you have little or no information and increase your knowledge.

But suppose your problem is the very opposite. Many people get bogged down in the middle of a project because they have so much information that they feel overwhelmed. Or they have too many ideas (even too many good ones). There is an optimum level of knowledge of course (it varies for different projects and for different people). Either too much or too little leads to a decrease in interest and involvement.

So if you are tired of collecting information or ideas, process what you have. Consider each item; then file it, condense it, throw it out, organize it. A particularly helpful step, if you've been gathering knowledge from books or other people or your own head, is to write something down. Even if it is no good for final use, it gives you something fresh to react to, or to show others to get their reactions.

The Cushion That Never Got Made

Ms. Gill had long wanted to make a needlepoint cushion for a favorite chair. She kept putting it off, because there seemed to be so many details to work out before she could even begin to think of putting needle to canvas. Finally, wisely realizing she would have to start somewhere if she was going to get on with it, she went shopping for materials. She spent several weeks looking for the perfect pattern and yarns. A saleslady at one store talked her into taking a month-long intensive course on the history and technology of needlepoint. Having completed the course, she decided that the only way to have yarns of the precise colors she wanted was to get them from a mail-order house. This led to a six-week delay while she inquired about samples, received some, asked for more, received those, and finally made her choice.

Then, having assembled her materials, she realized she did not have the right place to work on her needlepoint project. So she decided to fix up the spare room, change the lighting fixtures, clean out the accumulation of old junk, etc. Another month went by. Then she asked her husband to make her a special box for her supplies, since she did not like any of the types she saw in the stores. Another two-week delay. When at long last she had taken care of every conceivable detail, eliminated all risk of error or inconvenience, and laid everything out in great orderliness, she had become so sick of the whole thing that she thought she had best delay a while before starting.

The moral of the story is: You can become so carried away with preparatory steps that you beat any project to death. I said before that *any* task is acceptable as a stimulus change so long as it bears some relation to the Overwhelming A-1. But it must also be relatively short and easy. It must lead you toward the completion of the A-1. If Ms. Gill's A-1 was to turn loose her curiosity about needlepoint and follow wherever it led, then she accomplished her A-1 in fine style. But if it was to make a new cushion for her chair, then she certainly went astray.

Any major project, such as adding a new wing to your house, or introducing an important new procedure in your office, is a prolonged effort that requires continuing involvement at many stages. This takes large blocks of time.

First schedule the time needed to work on the project: Then when the time comes use the ideas in this chapter to keep involved.

17. SOMETIMES IT PAYS TO SLOW DOWN

IN SOME SITUATIONS, such techniques as instant tasks and stimulus change will not halt procrastination, because you harbor a too-active dislike or distaste for the A-1. Talking to your child's teacher about a bad grade, seeing the doctor for an annual checkup, asking the bank for a loan, drawing up a new will, going for a job interview—these are all examples of important but unpleasant tasks that many people put off. You probably include them when you plan, and underscore their importance by assigning them an A-priority. But when the time comes to follow through, the task looms up larger than life in all its unpleasantness, and you hastily turn to some other activity instead.

A decision to turn from an unpleasant A-1 to a more pleasant task gets far less time and rational consideration than it deserves. Typically, such a decision is made quickly, often in a matter of a few seconds.

Suppose you take out a letter you should answer now. Writing a reply is your A-1, but since it involves admitting an embarrassing mistake you find the task distasteful. You lay the letter aside for the third time this week and pick up a magazine instead. Soon you're absorbed in an interesting article, and have forgotten all about the unpleasant letter. The sequence of steps that led to your procrastinating on the A-1 took no more than fifteen seconds.

Let's back up and look at that decision more closely. You already had a clearly identified A-1. The next step was to do it. But you hesitated. In essence, you had two choices at this point. You could.

(1) do the A-1, thereby making the best use of your time;
(2) do something else, thereby wasting your time.

True, you got *some* value out of the activity you turned to instead of the A-1, but since the A-1 was the best use of your time, the other activity was a comparative waste of time.

What can you do when you have no doubt that you should do the unpleasant A-1, yet are strongly inclined to run away from it and turn to something else?

First, you must recognize clearly when you have reached such a pivotal point. You're at Decision Time when you're at the point of choosing whether to do the A-1 now or to avoid it. It is somewhat like being at the top of a mountain. There are two paths leading down the mountain, one to the north and one to the south. Once you take a few steps you will be on your way down one side of the mountain. But for the moment you are poised at the top, uncommitted.

Once you realize you're at Decision Time, you'll want to take control of the decisionmaking process. The way to do this is to *slow down* the final decision. A quick decision to put the unpleasant A-1 out of sight and mind gives you little chance to curb your tendency to procrastinate. Take enough time to consider the situation carefully. Give yourself every opportunity *not* to ditch the A-1 for some activity of lesser value. Slow down the process so that you have time to make a conscious and deliberate choice.

Take the case of the unanswered letter. When you catch yourself putting the letter aside, slow your hand down. If you take a full minute to put the letter away, instead of the second or two you would normally take, you'll be forced to confront your thoughts about the letter. You'll have enough time to review why you've been putting the letter aside, and try to come up with a better way to solve your dilemma than by procrastination.

Have you ever done anything you didn't like? Of course you have. Everyone has. In childhood your parents insisted that you go to bed at 7:30 P.M., even though it was summer vacation and the older kids were still outside playing Hide-and-Seek. On April 15 you mailed your income-tax check to Uncle Sam, even though you would rather have used the money to buy a four-track stereo for the den. You studied for an exam coming up in a subject you loathe. The list is endless.

Even as you do something you don't like, you have a choice. You can do it grudgingly or, having decided to do it now, you can do it cheerfully. Why make yourself miserable? Once you've decided to do a task, you may as well do the best you can and try to enjoy yourself.

If you sense you're about to avoid the A-1 and do something else instead, tell yourself quite emphatically that you're at Decision Time. Remind yourself what an important time it is. Caution yourself to slow down. Now use these three ways to help you overcome your distaste for the A-1:

(1) *Deal with the unpleasantness directly.*

(2) *Recognize the greater unpleasantness that results from delay.*

(3) *Create enthusiasm that counterbalances the unpleasantness.*

I'll deal with each of these in detail. Once you have all three in your toolkit, you can use whichever seems most appropriate to give you the extra push you need at Decision Time for doing the A-1 now.

18. DON'T LET FEAR GET IN YOUR WAY

How MANY TIMES have you avoided doing something important because you were afraid of making a mistake? Or getting angry? Or feeling guilty? Or hurting yourself or others? Or being rejected? Or taking on too much responsibility? Or confronting the unknown? Lots of times, I'm sure.

I'm not a psychiatrist, so it would be presumptuous of me to make any diagnosis, especially at long distance, of anyone's particular emotional hang-up. The techniques I discuss in this chapter work in a bypass fashion; they are not intended to cure anyone of any particular emotional problem, but to allow him to function while he either works his problem out himself or gets professional help.

I'll deal primarily with fear, because my conversations with psychiatrists and psychologists have convinced me that fear is at the root of all avoidance. If you can conquer your fear, you can do that unpleasant A-1.

I have encountered many cases of people avoiding a task to which they have assigned a high priority because subconsciously they feared the consequences that would follow once the task was completed.

The sales executive mentioned earlier kept procrastinating on his A-1 of trying to sell a new account because of his fear of adding further to his workload if he were successful. His fear needed to be allayed by clearing away some of his other work; only then did he stop avoiding his high-priority A and go after that big account.

A supervisor was asked to develop a procedure manual for a job that he had always personally directed. His boss made it very clear that the manual had a higher priority than anything else. Again and again the supervisor put the task at the head of his To Do List, yet he did nothing about working on the manual. Finally he realized he was procrastinating out of fear that if he finished the procedure manual, he might eventually be out of a job. He would no longer be indispensable. His real A-1 was a talk with his boss to clarify what his status would be once the job on the manual was done.

Don't let your emotions do you in. If you suspect you are avoiding the A-1 because of some fear, then at Decision Time ask yourself, "What am I afraid of?" Make a list of possibilities and single out the fear that is most likely causing the avoidance. Then confront that fear head on. How? Take the case of Mr. Blue.

Mr. Blue was a sales representative for an industrial-products firm. He knew that the best use of his time was to develop contacts with as many new purchasing agents as possible. Nevertheless, he always stretched out his visits to those agents who were old friends, even though many of them could repay him only in talk and not in profit. He avoided making calls on new agents, because they occasionally rejected him or treated him rudely.

Now Mr. Blue had prepared an annual sales plan. It rightly emphasized new agent contacts, but from the very first day he tried to implement the plan, he found himself running away. His fear of feeling rejected was clearly preventing him from following through on his wonderful plan.

Determined to find some solution to his dilemma, Mr. Blue decided to focus on one particular goal—to see the purchasing agent from the Ajax Company. He'd long wanted to go after the Ajax account. The chance of actually closing this sale was truly exciting. But he was scared that the agent might turn him down with some devastating comment, and then he would be worse off than before.

How to Extinguish Fear

As he contemplated the telephone call to the Ajax agent and felt fear holding him back, Mr. Blue told himself that being afraid was silly; that there was nothing to worry about; that he had more important things to do than worrying. In effect, he said to his fear, "Go away, you're bothering me." This had often helped him over the hump he confronted before making a call to a new agent, but since he had particularly strong feelings about this agent, his pep talk was not a sufficient antidote.

If Mr. Blue's fear had been at a low-enough level—of campfire rather than forest fire proportions—then it could probably have been easily extinguished. But with an out-of-control fear, a really threatening emotion, such a solution rarely works. Indeed Mr. Blue's current predicament was such that when he told himself, "There's nothing to fear," it only made matters worse. Not only was he afraid; he was afraid that he was afraid when he shouldn't be afraid! He certainly had to find some other way of handling his fear of being rejected by the Ajax agent.

How to Contain Fear

A small fire can easily be put out with a little water, but if a fire is raging uncontrollably, it's best to contain it, to create boundaries and then in effect say to the fire, "You can burn all you want inside this circle, but you may not cross this line!"

Mr. Blue found that although he could not extinguish his fear, he was able to contain it, at least for the moment. He realized that he might not even get to talk to the feared agent, but only to his secretary. Anyway, he thought he'd be able to survive a quick, clean "No" over the telephone. If he did succeed in making an appointment, there would be plenty to worry about, so he would give himself lots of time to indulge his fears—but only after he made the call.

At this point Mr. Blue recalled the character Major Major in the novel *Catch-22*, who announced that he was not to be disturbed when he was in, and that visitors were to be shown into his office only when he was out. Mr. Blue wasted a few more seconds daydreaming about how nice it would be if new agents were never in when he called. Then he came back to reality, hoped that the man would not be in, and dialed the number.

It turned out that the Ajax agent was in, and could see Mr. Blue the following Monday at 2:30 P.M., four days away.

At first the exhilaration that came from actually having gotten the appointment kept Mr. Blue busy all afternoon, lining up other appointments with new agents.

But the next morning, when he should have been collecting data and assembling material for the Ajax presentation, Mr.

Blue found himself procrastinating once more. He kept turning to other, far less important matters, and in between he fretted about the grueling questions the agent would ask. As his fear of failure gathered momentum, he envisioned himself appearing foolish and ill-prepared. When he could stand his painful imaginings no longer, he escaped to the coffee machine down the hall.

How to "Judo" Your Fear

At this point Mr. Blue could neither extinguish his fear nor contain it; he had to face the situation head on. As he returned to his desk he recalled another strategy he could resort to—using judo to throw his fear. The idea behind judo, he knew, is to use your opponent's own strength and weight against him, thereby turning potential defeat into victory. Mr. Blue's fear was coming at him with great force and effect. He would have to throw that fear by using its force to his advantage, rather than letting it do him in.

As he sat down at his desk his inner dialogue went something like this:

FEAR: "I am going to make a fool of myself. I really don't know much about the Ajax Company or how they can best use my products . . ."

JUDO: ". . . if that's the case, then I better put some time into finding out more about Ajax right away."

FEAR: "Then there are all those questions I know he'll ask . . ."

JUDO: ". . . and instead of worrying about being ill-prepared, I had better try to anticipate his questions and dig up the answers right now."

With his energy more positively channeled, Mr. Blue gulped down the last of his coffee and started to research the Ajax account. Everytime something unpleasant about the upcoming interview occurred to him, he "judoed" it. When he thought of a terrible mistake he might make, he made a mental note not to let *that* happen. His fear actually spurred him on, since he realized that only conscientious work might save him. There was no procrastinating the rest of Friday; he wanted to be sure he was prepared.

Monday afternoon, on the way over to the Ajax Company,

he started worrying again. By the time he entered the building he was shaking all over. All his efforts on Friday would be wasted if his fear kept him from being able to think straight.

Ballooning Your Fears

At this point Mr. Blue's fear could not be dealt with by any of the strategies I have discussed so far. After all, this was it! If ever there was a good time to be afraid, it was now. Mr. Blue realized that his only chance was to give in to his fears completely and hope that they would burn themselves out before it was too late.

As he got into the elevator, he asked himself, "What's the worst thing that could possibly happen to me as a result of this visit?" Perhaps the agent would call his boss and tell him that Mr. Blue was incompetent. Perhaps he would tell all his friends Mr. Blue was an idiot and they should never do business with him.

Getting warmed up, Mr. Blue began to balloon his fears even more. His fantasies were easily the equal of Walter Mitty's. Perhaps the agent would organize a boycott of Mr. Blue's products. Perhaps the agent would start a smear campaign against him and he would be spurned everywhere by everyone. With no safe territory left, Mr. Blue pictured that he would withdraw to a storage closet and starve to death, uncared for, completely and finally rejected.

Mr. Blue got off the elevator, walked slowly down the corridor, and was outside the agent's door when he realized that his fears had carried him into complete absurdity. The balloon burst. The situation could not possibly be as terrible as he had imagined. Having envisioned himself at the point of death, he had nowhere to go but up. With a last nervous shake, he opened the door.

In fact, nothing terrible happened. The agent was in, welcomed Mr. Blue warmly, thanked him for coming over, and inquired why Mr. Blue had not come in to see him sooner. He listened attentively as Mr. Blue delivered his well-prepared presentation, said he was certainly interested and then and there gave him a small order as a starter. Mr. Blue left his office and breathed a great sigh of relief.

In time, partly because of the confidence that comes from successes, but also because he survived the occasional inevitable rejections intact, he began to look forward to encounters with new agents as a way of testing himself and reaffirming his inner strength. He gradually came to disassociate his sense of worth as a person from the role he played as a salesman. The agents who turned him down were not rejecting him, they were rejecting his product. This change in attitude did not happen right away; in fact, it took Mr. Blue two years to reduce his fear of rejection to an occasional twinge.

I should point out that Mr. Blue has behaved as all good examples in books behave—he has managed to exhibit a number of problems in dealing with fear, and he has benefited from all the techniques I suggested using.

I wouldn't expect you to do as well the very first time you try to conquer fears you've built up over the years. But the next time you suspect that some fear is causing you to procrastinate on a A-1, try extinguishing, containing, judoing, and ballooning that fear until it is afraid to show itself ever again.

19. THE REAL PRICE OF DELAY

WHEN YOU'RE AT DECISION TIME and suspect you're about to procrastinate on an unpleasant A-1, taking a moment to contemplate the consequences of delay can often get you back on the track. Let me tell you about a woman who hated to write thank-you notes.

Anne Davis receives a birthday gift from out of town. She tells herself that she must take a few minutes right away and drop Aunt Mary a note. A few lines will do: "I got the sweater. It looks beautiful and is just my size. Thank you so very much."

But Ms. Davis, being something of a perfectionist, really doesn't want to settle for such an insipid note—she'd like to write something with more verve. After all, she doesn't want Aunt Mary to think that her four years of college were a total waste! She doesn't feel up to being eloquent at the moment (and, of course, she has a hundred other things to do), so she puts off thanking Aunt Mary for now.

Two weeks pass before she faces up to the fact that she still has not written to Aunt Mary. By this time, she figures, Aunt Mary is getting somewhat impatient. Well, she'll make up for the delay by sending off a charming two-page letter telling her all about how often she wears the sweater, how well it goes with several of her skirts, how comfortable it is, and how many compliments she has received from friends. She doesn't have time to write such a long letter now . . . but she tells herself she'll be sure to get around to it very soon.

Two more weeks go by, and now Ms. Davis is feeling very angry with herself. She is so ashamed, and so afraid of what Aunt Mary must think of her. Surely she'll tell everyone in the family what a lazy, ungrateful niece she has! Ms. Davis will have to think up some pretty good excuses. "Everytime I sit down to write you, the phone rings," or "This has been the busiest month of my life" will perhaps do the trick.

Hopefully, if she fills her letter with enough personal anecdotes about her hectic life, Aunt Mary will forgive her.

How the Problem Escalates

At this point, writing the thank-you note has become *very* important and *very* unpleasant. It's not surprising that Ms. Davis hates writing thank-you notes! She starts worrying about the letter whenever she has an odd moment. She constructs the note in her head while taking a shower and while taking out the garbage, but this doesn't bring her any closer to getting the letter *written*.

Ms. Davis starts feeling terribly guilty—so guilty, in fact, the thought of the letter makes her sick. In order to avoid this, she now blocks out of her mind any thought of the unwritten note.

Finally one day the unwritten note comes back to haunt her, and Ms. Davis acknowledges to herself that it is *Decision Time*. Should she: (1) write a ten-page letter bringing Aunt Mary up-to-date on life with the Davis family for the last two years, and off-handedly sneak in a thank-you for the sweater? (2) wait another nine months and if Aunt Mary sends another birthday present (hopefully she won't!) thank her for both presents at the same time? (3) pretend she never received the sweater? (4) wait until she goes back home for a visit, and then impress Aunt Mary with how she remembered the sweater after all these years and was waiting to thank her in person? (5) telephone Aunt Mary long-distance and after a half an hour of chit-chat (at considerable cost) to soften her up, thank her? or (6) give up any hope of ever being able to face Aunt Mary again because how can she ever explain why she couldn't find five minutes to write a quick note the week the sweater arrived?

What Is the Price of Delay?

Ms. Davis's delay in thanking Aunt Mary cost her many minutes of anguish. She would have suffered less had she slowed down and made a deliberate effort to recall the consequences of her past delays: Her Aunt had felt slighted before and her own mother had written an admonishing letter about it. She knew from prior experience how each week of procrastination in writing a thank-you note escalated both the size of the task and the discomfort level. How much better to write the note now than to endure such suffering again.

Before you consider delaying in such situations, slow down. Take a minute or two to consider the consequences that will follow.

Acknowledge that if past experience and present resolve are any indication, this is not something that will go away. You *are* going to do this task eventually. The question is not "Will I do it?" but "When?" Ask yourself, "Since I am going to do it eventually, do I really want to pay the price of delay?"

What is this price you'll have to pay? While it's different in various situations, the following guidelines are generally true.

For one thing, if a task is not something that will go away, the actual work required may increase as time passes (as with the thank-you note). Also, it will keep haunting you until you do it. Here are some other situations where procrastination creates trouble and extra work. You can:

put off filing your paperwork so long that every time you need a piece of paper you have to hunt through a huge "to be filed" stack,

delay changing your car's motor oil until you need a $375 engine repair two months after the manufacturer's guarantee expires,

put off sweeping crumbs from the back of the pantry so that you come home one day to find your crumbs gone and thousands of ants in their place,

delay action of replacing the unreliable widget section until suddenly you are swamped with customer complaints and must spend more time answering complaints than fixing the widget section would ever have taken—and you still have to fix the widget section.

Even when the task seems to remain identical whether you do it now or later, its impact on you can be substantially different.

Suppose you feel so tense and nervous about asking your boss for a raise that you put it off until tomorrow. Tomorrow, when you think about it again, you feel every bit as anxious, if not more so. And every time you think about it, you not only remind yourself what a nasty scene you may provoke by your request, but you summon up all the emotions associated with this nastiness. In other words, every time you think about the task and put it off, you suffer some of the same pain as if you had actually done it.

You still don't know whether you'll get a raise, so you'll have to think about it further and again suffer pain. Moreover, there is a tendency for your anxiety to increase each time you think about it. Does it make sense to put off doing something because you feel tense and nervous about it—and then feel tense and nervous anyway?

Next time you're tempted to procrastinate on an unpleasant A-1, slow down. Why suffer all the pain associated with thinking about it and get none of the benefits? You've survived every nasty situation you've faced. Sometimes—be honest now—didn't you worry unnecessarily? Didn't some of those experiences turn out to be tolerable and even occasionally pleasant? And even when there was real discomfort, didn't it often stop quicker than you had imagined?

Consider the Risks

Can you really afford to risk delaying a large, important project until the last minute? Suppose you aren't feeling well when the last minute comes? Or you face an unexpectedly large number of unavoidable interruptions? Or another crisis comes up that must be dealt with immediately? Or the project turns out to require more hours than you had originally estimated? When you delay a project until close to the deadline there is always the risk that you'll run short of time and have to submit inadequate work or miss the deadline.

The college student who assesses the risk of delay has to decide whether his term paper is an A, B, or C priority. The student who is more interested in dates, sports, politics or recreational reading might well give the term paper a C-priority until the last minute, but he pays the price when his professor gives the paper only a C-grade.

Many people say, "I deliberately put things off until the last minute because I know I work best under pressure. If I wait until the deadline is really close, I'm more effective. I waste less time, I get better ideas. I don't lose by delay; I gain!"

If you've made a clear-headed assessment of your work habits and are convinced that such is the case, I say, fine! Many people *do* work best under pressure. For others, too much pressure can be devastating. Whether you're a college student putting off a term paper until the last minute, a homemaker putting off packing valuable china and stemware for the move to the new house, or an executive putting off preparing your fall sales campaign, you must assess your own work habits and determine how you function best.

Do you really work *well* under pressure? Consider the college student with his term-paper problem. There are a number of reasons why the quality of his work is not as likely to be as high as if he had more time. Valuable reference material or interviews may be left out because of time pressures. Ideas that require investigation cannot be explored when there's no time to investigate. A last-minute effort means that accuracy may have to be dispensed with. No rewriting is possible and so the prose style will suffer.

Ask yourself if you perhaps spend *more* time by delaying until the last minute? Working overtime on a crash program leads to physical and mental fatigue. Thinking becomes fuzzy. Hours may be lost solving a problem that a clear mind could penetrate in minutes.

Emotions may eat up extra time, too. It takes time to worry about whether you're ever going to start the project; whether your work is going to be good enough; whether you're going to make the deadline. Do you feel anger at yourself for putting yourself in such a position? Regret at not being able to go to a show tonight? Disappointment that you're really not giving yourself a chance to show your ability to do good work under more favorable circumstances?

The Drawbacks of Pressure

The need to expedite routine parts of a project when every minute counts often forces you to do work yourself which could have been done by others had you budgeted your time better. You'll have to do the typing, photocopying, collating, stapling, and other clerical work, because there's no secretary at 3 A.M. to help you.

Besides, do you *like* working well under pressure? Or do you feel a slave to deadlines? Do you experience last-minute panic about whether or not you will finish an important project on time? Do you wonder if there isn't some other way—a relaxed, in-control-of-the-situation approach?

Do you find that you behave badly toward other people when you're under pressure? Do you make other people miserable by your demands for priority of your work over theirs? Remember, people may not think *your* project is the most important.

If your backlog and new demands continually create pressure without letup and you don't like it, perhaps you're in the wrong job. But if the pressure is self-inflicted by your own perpetual procrastination, then maybe you can do something about it.

Do you work well *only* under pressure? Maybe you thrive on the feeling of exhilaration that comes from the total involvement demanded in meeting a last-minute deadline. But what happens when the pressure is off? Do you find the time between deadlines woefully flat and stale? Puttering around, shuffling papers, doing trivia and giving the pressure a chance to build up isn't much fun. True, you can use the time between deadlines to goof off, recover from the last crisis, prepare yourself for the next crisis—which is all to the good. But if you feel you're fully alive only when under great pressure, and feel let down in the in-between periods, then you may want to try some changes. Ideally, you want to be flexible enough to make good use of your time whatever the situation.

Here's a suggestion to help you avoid deadline mania: Don't wait quite so long before plunging in. Give yourself a little more lead time before the deadline. Try to start a little sooner, even though the pressure is not full-blown. As you learn to decrease the amount of pressure you need to work well, I think you'll find that you're increasing your willpower. You'll find you've gained a new sense of freedom and self-confidence. You'll feel more relaxed and in control of your time (and your life).

20. LEARN TO STRESS THE BENEFITS

I'M NOW GOING to describe a technique called "Stress the Benefits" to help you muster enthusiasm at Decision Time for any unappetizing A-1.

Consider Mr. O'Henry, who had an idea that he thought would save his organization several thousand dollars a year. Normally he would have submitted his idea immediately to his company's suggestion system. But this time he delayed submitting his proposal, because he knew that, if adopted, it might mean cutting back on the work assigned to one of his co-workers.

The improvement Mr. O'Henry envisioned was tricky. There was a certain amount of risk involved. His supervisor had already given his opinion on the suggestion: "We tried that nine years ago. It didn't work then and it won't work now."

The risk of failure, the possible resentment of his co-worker, and the hassle with his supervisor had kept him from formally presenting his suggestion until now. Still, Mr. O'Henry was convinced that, everything considered, submitting his proposal was the A-1.

He managed finally to sell himself on submitting the proposal by listing all the benefits he could expect. The benefits were of two types: (1) pluses that would start when the A-1 was done and (2) minuses that would stop when the A-1 was done.

The pluses included the following: a cash bonus of 20 percent of the first year's savings (at least $1,250), self-satisfaction for a well done, and recognition from the management (leading to promotion, more interesting and enjoyable work, and a higher salary).

The minuses that would stop when the A-1 was done included: worrying every night about whether to submit the suggestion form (worry *could* lead to ulcers, spending time in hospital, using savings to pay hospital bills, etc.), avoiding his co-worker because of ambivalent feelings toward him, hating his supervisor for blocking his progress in the company.

Once he started to Stress the Benefits, the A-1 began to look so attractive that he was able to put possible drawbacks out of his mind, and go eagerly on with the suggestion form.

How to Reward Yourself

It's particularly valuable to Stress the Benefits as you plow through a long or complex job. Sometimes it's even necessary to exaggerate (balloon) the benefits in the middle of a hard A-1.

If you've already considered all the benefits you'll reap from the A-1 and still find yourself having a hard time accomplishing it, then you may have to try adding outside benefits. The new benefits are like a rider to a Congressional bill that contains "sweeteners" to induce wavering Congressmen to vote for the bill.

Suppose you have to go on a business trip. It's particularly unappealing to you. You may be able to make it more palatable by tacking a few days on the end of your trip to take your wife to that ski resort you've been thinking of visiting. You've gone beyond stressing the normal benefits (more money, possible promotion, etc.). You've added a "rider" to inspire you to do your A-1—take that very important business trip.

You can give yourself a reward for working on a task as a way to coax yourself along. Plan to work until eleven o'clock and then take a break to read the news magazine you've been waiting to look at—or sleep late the next morning.

Give yourself a reward when you reach various milestones along the way of a larger project: when all the data for a survey comes; after you've interviewed six people to replace your assistant; after you've got a first draft of the plans for the new plant. If you work on the annual report today, you're entitled to go out for a drink after work. These are all ways of rewarding yourself.

Rewards on final completion are important too. After I finish writing this book I'll take a vacation.

It also helps to relate an immediate reward to your Lifetime Goals. You can say, "Well, now, if I do this I'm going to keep my job, and I'm going to get promoted." Then you can build up the reward in your mind. If you have a good set of Lifetime Goals you can probably think of many more connections between doing this A-1 and achieving some Lifetime Goals. Again, you're Stressing the Benefits.

Another way of keeping the value of the task in front of you is to give yourself a little taste in advance of what will happen if you do keep working on the A-1. Remember that vacation I have promised myself for when I finish my book? Well, long before I actually finish I'll go down to our travel agent and make the airline, hotel, and car-rental reservations. Then I'll go back and keep on writing. I get further along on my A-1 by Stressing the Benefits.

Another way to get yourself to do unpleasant A-1's is to turn the whole task into a game. Let's say painting your living room took you and your wife ten hours four years ago. Have you improved with age? See if you can shave some time off that ten hours. If you're a secretary with a particular report to be done every so often, see if you can type it flawlessly this time. Keep a little piece of paper noting how many errors you made last time and see if you can beat that score.

If it's a rather routine job, see how much of it you can knock off in fifteen minutes, or how nonchalant you can be while doing it. Anything that will help you get the task done is valuable. It helps you complete the task by varying the incentive, and even artificial incentives can help. Stress the Benefits and move closer to getting the A-1 done.

21. HOW TO GET BACK AFTER YOU'VE ESCAPED

IN all my discussion of procrastination I've assumed that, once you've done a good job of planning, you're clear in your own mind about what your A-1 is. You may go right ahead and do it or you may not. My clients have found that the techniques I've explained in the last several chapters will significantly increase the will to "do it now" and throttle down procrastination.

But still, everyone procrastinates on occasion. So now I'd like to show you what is really happening when you *don't* do the A-1, when you deliberately or not-so-deliberately decide to put off the really important activity.

If you're not doing the A-1, you're doing something else instead. This "something else," whatever its intrinsic value (which may be very high), is in part appealing because it is an Escape from doing or thinking about the A-1.

Everyone has favorite Escapes. Escapes can be A's, B's, C's, or watching the girls go by. If you're at work, an Escape generally needs to be something that gives others the impression that you're busy and productive. In a private office or at home you have somewhat more leeway. You can even take a nap.

Seven Common Mistakes

Here is a run-down of some of the most common Escapes. As you read through them, ask yourself how many of these escape routes you use when running away from the A-1.

Indulging yourself. Doing something you really enjoy. Buying a new hat or tie or book. Taking the rest of the day off to play golf. Getting a suntan. Going to the movies. Sleeping. Taking a bath or shower and leisurely grooming yourself.

Socializing. Visiting with others. Lingering on the telephone. Renewing an acquaintance with an old friend. Making small talk every chance you get.

Reading. Catching up on the backlog of unread periodicals stacked on the side table. Skimming through material previously relegated to a bottom drawer as not really worth reading. Spending two hours on *The Wall Street Journal*, or trying to make a dent in your pile of unread copies of the Sunday *New York Times* or Book-of-the-Month Club selections.

Doing it yourself. Baking your own bread. Spending an hour taking notes on a reference book rather than photocopying the three essential pages. Adding a long string of numbers by hand rather than walking over to the adding machine. Doing something that could be delegated. Spending your time solving other people's problems. Delving into aspects of the job that don't really concern you.

Overdoing it. Supervising employees so closely that they can't get their work done. Keeping every visitor an extra fifteen minutes while you talk about your mimosa, butterfly collection, arthritis, or lack of time. Being so diligent in giving your boss progress reports that you have little time to make progress. Rearranging your desk, inside and out, to be the very model of neatness and efficiency.

Running away. If you're in headquarters, organizing a field trip. If in the field, going to headquarters. Expediting something that doesn't need it: hand-carrying a memo to another branch office; paying your telephone bill in person. Taking a long coffee break; extending your lunch hour; taking time for a cocktail or shopping.

Daydreaming. Planning how you're going to spend your weekend. Worrying about all the things left undone at work. Wondering how you're going to spend the extra money from your hoped-for promotion. Recalling what a witty remark you made at a party yesterday.

No doubt you can add to this list some of your own special favorites. Please remember, I'm not saying that there is anything wrong with indulging yourself, reading, socializing, daydreaming. Quite the contrary; much of the fun in life comes from such things. Indeed, that is precisely why they are so appealing. The problem is you're trained to these escapes *when* you should be doing the A-1.

Other Escapes are more subtle and less readily recognized as such. Perhaps you dabble around the periphery of the A-1, spending too much time on irrelevant details rather than going to the heart of the matter. Or as Ms. Gill did with her needlepoint project, you spend so much time getting ready to begin the A-1 that you have no time left to do it.

Finally, there are what might be called the Emotional Escapes: feeling guilty, getting angry, worrying. Indulging in such feelings is a very common way of escaping from the A-1. To ask yourself whether perhaps you took the wrong job, married the wrong spouse, or bought the wrong house may well be useful. But if you *wallow* in such thoughts, it's time to ask Lakein's Question.

Admit When You're Wasting Time

Some Escapes are undoubtedly worth doing and are excellent uses of time: getting organized, making lists, improving morale, socializing, taking the day off, doing the A-2 or A-3, catching up on reading. Therefore, it is easy to tell yourself you're really making good use of your time, even though you are not doing the A-1. And perhaps you are. But you're not making the *best* use of your time.

The *best* use of your time—as you've already decided—is to do the A-1. Anything else is a comparative waste of time.

Consider one of my clients, a research scientist. He kept procrastinating on a difficult research study that had a very high priority. Despite his efforts to get involved and to convince himself how important it was, he kept stalling. At my suggestion, he began to take a careful look at each Decision Time when he chose to avoid the A-1 and turned to something else.

At first, he felt like a helpless observer. It seemed as if the procrastination process was operating in spite of anything he could do. Rather than be discouraged at this point, he consoled himself with the knowledge that he was trying to understand the dynamics of the process, which is the first step toward controlling it.

After several days of closely watching his actions at Decision Time, he found certain patterns emerging. The thought of doing the A-1 was always followed immediately by feelings of inadequacy and tension. Most of the time he then quickly turned to making improvements on an old and familiar research problem. He would talk to someone about some aspect of this other study, or rethink and rewrite portions that needed polishing. He felt completely on top of the situation. He was not doing the A-1, but he was doing something important and productive.

In the back of his mind, however, was the nagging thought that he was rationalizing. He was not perfecting the old report because it was essential (it *was* worth doing, but not now). He was doing it because it provided an easy Escape from the A-1.

On my recommendation, every time he found himself working on the old project he repeated silently over and over to himself, "I'm wasting my time." During the next week or so he admitted to himself dozens of times "I'm wasting my time."

At first, saying this didn't stop him from turning to an Escape. Then the words began to make a difference. He acknowledged that he really *was* wasting his time. The benefits he before associated with doing the Escape tasks had now lost much of their appeal.

As he realized more and more that he was wasting his own time, the tide began to change. Instead of letting the procrastination process run him, he told himself that he didn't *have* to waste his time. Just as he had chosen to do Escapes, he could choose to do the A-1. It really was a black and white choice—Escape vs. the A-1. As he became able to see his problem in these terms he began to reject Escape and zeroed in on the A-1 with increasing frequency.

The real payoff came when, several months later, a new and even more difficult research study was offered to him. Having learned how his Escape mechanism worked, he was able to stop procrastinating and get involved in the new project almost immediately.

I've found that saying over and over "I'm wasting my time" works very well for women who choose ever-present routine household chores over some challenging project they have included in their Lifetime Goals Statement. If a woman really wants to play the piano, every time she dusts the piano she should admit to herself, "I am wasting my time." If you use the "I'm wasting my time" warning signal, you will find it increasingly difficult to rationalize detours. Above all, you'll accept that it's *you* who is in control and makes the choices.

Even when you achieve a high level of control, so that your chances of choosing the A-1 at Decision Time are good, you won't always succeed. But if you can recognize when you are wasting your time, you'll definitely increase your chances further.

How to Cut Off Your Escape Routes

Another way to make sure you'll choose the A-1 at Decision Time is to cut off all your Escape routes. The principle is simple and is often used by people who are trying to lose weight or stop smoking. If you keep all candy or cigarettes out of the house, you make it that much harder to give in to the craving for them. Every time you crave candy or a cigarette after dinner, you have to make a special trip to the store. Your reluctance to bundle up to go out in the cold may exceed your longing for candy or a cigarette.

Should you perhaps cancel the subscription to the mediocre magazine you always turn to as an Escape from the A-1? If you can't bring yourself to that, how about hiding it in a drawer? At least then it won't have as much chance of distracting you as when it's sitting on your desk.

If you're a housewife and your mornings are full of A's that never seem to get done, then tactfully avoid your coffee-mate across the court. Sure, it's great fun talking to her but this delightful Escape prevents you from accomplishing the A-1.

Perhaps your downfall is the two-martini lunch that renders you useless for the balance of the afternoon. If the most important thing you can do is have lunch and a few drinks while you regale an important client then by all means do it; it's your A-1. But if it's really an Escape from something important you have to do this afternoon, then it might be a good idea to think twice. As a compromise, why not go to lunch with a teetotaler? That way you can still enjoy lunch. You'll probably moderate your alcoholic intake, allowing you to go after that A-1 this afternoon.

If your Escape is going to the supermarket three times a week, make it a rule that you'll go only once. To make sure that you really won't need to go, do something concrete about those meal-planning, stocking and freezing ideas you've been contemplating for years. If you forget something or run out, try to make do.

The Great Escape for nearly everybody is television. Liberate yourself! Give your set away and then stalk your A-1!

One final suggestion along these lines: You might want to give your secretary a list of your favorite Escapes. Just the fact that you know she has the list may prevent you from utilizing these dodges except in the most severe cases.

You Can Procrastinate Positively

It's just possible that you've tried all the suggestions I've made about how to stop procrastinating—without success. O.K. If you have to procrastinate, I'm going to show you how to do it positively.

Sit in a chair and do nothing. That's right—nothing. Don't read a book, don't shuffle papers, don't tackle your knitting, don't watch TV—just sit completely still.

If you sit doing nothing for fifteen or twenty minutes (don't cheat—you must do absolutely nothing), you should become very uneasy. That A-1 is staring you right in the face. And you're doing nothing. Precious minutes that you can use accomplishing a lifetime goal are slipping by. And you're sitting in a chair—doing nothing. Whenever I find myself procrastinating, this is the technique I use. Believe me, after ten minutes I'm off and running on my A-1.

22. HOW TO DO BETTER NEXT TIME

To get the most out of the suggestions and techniques I've described, a good deal of stick-to-itiveness or will-power is called for. You'll need willpower to:

(1) plan when you're feeling harried and overwhelmed;
(2) keep yourself involved in a project even though some of the instant tasks you try lead to a dead end;
(3) avoid your favorite Escapes when you have an important but unpleasant A-1 to do;
(4) maintain a positive attitude in spite of previous "failures";
(5) do something every day on your Lifetime Goals;
(6) overcome fears, real or imagined;
(7) resist doing a very easy (but unimportant) task that is right in front of you.

Everyone knows that "Where there's a will, there's a way." And everyone has some willpower. But how do you develop all the willpower you really need? I'll now show you how to take the willpower you already have and build on it so that it will be available to you when you need it most.

You probably did many things today even though you didn't want to do them: got up out of bed, caught the 7:51 to work, dictated that awkward letter, ordered the Diet Special at lunch, smiled cheerfully at Mrs. McPlump, who tried to tell you about her backache again, restrained your anger when your son came home with a rip in his best jacket, went to the PTA meeting when you really wanted to stay home out of the rain, held that yoga position an extra minute even though your foot cramped.

Try These Willpower-Building Exercises

We'll begin by doing some willpower-building exercises. At first we'll make them easy. The mistake most people make when they try to develop willpower is that they push too hard. When you go on a weight-lifting program, you don't start by lifting two-hundred-pound weights. If you'll set yourself easy tasks, you'll accomplish them. You wouldn't try to ride a bucking bronco if you didn't know how to ride a horse. Yet, you're making the same mistake if you try to gather enough willpower to lose thirty pounds off the bat. How about starting with three?

Good teachers know that children learn best when their work is at the proper level so they can make steady growth. Studies show that learning a new skill in industry is greatly facilitated if early efforts meet with success. The Royal Canadian Air Force exercises build gradually from day to day so that the exerciser is hardly aware of the increased effort required to do the next day's exercise; yet the cumulative effect over several months is significant.

Therefore, I suggest that if you want to increase your willpower you begin by practicing in easy situations before applying the willpower you're building to do more and more difficult tasks.

Normally, the only time when people consciously test their willpower is when they need it. But if you apply it only when the task is difficult and you need all the help you can get, it will not be surprising if you fail fairly often.

The will is like a wild horse. If you want to train a wild horse to do productive work, you obviously can't tame it by running away. You have to keep in contact with the horse. There's really only one way to succeed: To get on that horse and stay on. Try to ride it. You may have to pick yourself off the ground several times, but stick with it. The idea is to stay with it even if the horse is going in the wrong direction.

Suppose the horse is heading for its favorite spot far out in the pasture. It's on a course that will take it between two trees. You're not able to get it to do an about-face, but you may be able to alter its course. If you continue this process patiently, you'll eventually be able to get the horse to go where you want it to go. You now have it "under control." Having reached this stage, you can begin to turn its energy toward productive work.

Increasing your willpower is like taming a wild horse. The key is to move forward in gradual stages, as I shall explain. It's an easy procedure. Indeed, it may seem too easy. Don't discount its potency because it doesn't demand much of you at first. Try it, you'll like it! And what's more, you'll find it extremely valuable. Here how it works.

A person generally feels the need for willpower when he has rationally decided to do one thing, yet is strongly pushed or pulled by the desire to do something else instead. You plan to get up early and take an invigorating hike, but stay in bed instead. Or you decide to spend the evening writing letters instead of watching TV, but find yourself drawn away from the letters toward an interesting program. In the face of some desire to the contrary, sticking with your initial decision can be very difficult.

The next time you find yourself giving in to such a desire rather than persisting with your rational decision, make a clear mental note of it. Admit that you're the one who decided to stay in bed or to watch TV. Take credit for the "unwanted" decision.

Granted, the decision may not have been one over which you had much control—you may have been acting as much from compulsion as from choice. Still, you *did* make a decision of sorts, and it *did* lead you directly to some action.

How to Wean Yourself Away from TV

At this point you've changed nothing about your actions. You're still doing something contrary to what you want to do, and you can't stop yourself. Claim credit for the decision. Go ahead, don't be afraid. Recognize that your will was involved when you stayed in bed late or turned from your letters to the TV.

The first step is to train yourself to become less compulsive about "reflex" actions like watching television. But it's important to start small and selectively. Is there at least some part of the evening's entertainment you could give up?

You could decide that you'll turn down the sound during

all the deodorant, toothpaste, and aspirin commercials. It isn't long before the first toothpaste ad appears. True to your plan, you get up and turn the sound down. Then you get up again when the commercial is over and turn the sound up. You do this twice more and decide you're tired of bouncing up and down. You say to yourself, "I think this was a neat plan, but I *will not* turn the sound off any more tonight." After all, enough is enough. When the next commercial comes along, you just sit there and congratulate yourself on not getting up again.

The next day you begin again with the same plan, and this time you get up six times before pooping out. Again you refuse to turn the sound down after that. However, during a particularly obnoxious commercial about midnight you find yourself starting to get up again. Now *you cannot lose!* If you get up and turn it off, congratulate yourself on your willpower in going back to your original plan. If you do not turn it off, congratulate yourself on your willpower in resisting the desire to turn it off and sticking to your revised decision not to get up again.

Interpret whatever you do as exactly what you wanted to do. This shows you're truly in control of your actions.

The next night, try a different strategy. This time turn off every alternate bathroom products commercial. If you miss one, don't be the least concerned. Simply tell yourself, "I reserve the right to change my mind and I've decided that I'll make an exception in this case." Your making an exception also helps to demonstrate that you're not an inflexible machine but a thinking, feeling, spontaneous person. Be proud of it! Interpret all your actions as positive, as exactly what you want to do.

After a couple of weeks, turn the sound up and down on other kinds of commercials (margarine, coffee, automobile). You're beginning to become more aware of how many different kinds of commercials there are and how annoying they can be. You're also starting to suspect that there must be a lot of things around that are more fun than watching TV commercials. You can confirm this if you experiment by listening carefully to every word of every commercial the next night without exception. Notice how much willpower you've built up to be able to listen closely to something that you are now really beginning to dislike.

One of my clients was particularly ingenious in developing his willpower while watching TV. In his first experiments he deliberately waited a few seconds until after the commercial was over and he did not turn the sound back up until after the program had actually resumed. He gradually extended this soundless time from two seconds to five and then to fifteen. Next he experimented with turning the whole set off when a bathroom product commercial came on, and read a magazine while it was off. Sometimes he decided to finish reading the page before returning to a program that was not one of his favorites. He continued experimenting and enlarging his area of freedom and the muscle of his willpower. He started turning the set on later and later in the evening. Within six weeks he was able to turn the set off during half-hour segments which he knew from past experience would only be disappointing programs. And all this time his ability to acquire increased control over his time-wasting urges made him feel better about himself.

When you attempt to develop your willpower remember: don't try to push yourself too far, between extending your capabilities gradually and stretching yourself so far that you break. Don't push yourself beyond your limits of endurance. Think in terms of extending your capabilities gradually, rather than stretching yourself to the breaking point.

A Couple of Extra Minutes Help

After you demonstrate your willpower in little ways, on little tasks, on easy things, turn gradually to more difficult ones. If you must confront a very difficult task, don't be concerned with conquering it. Be satisfied if you put up a little better fight than you might have six months ago. When you develop willpower, time is on your side if you improve just a little every day.

Gradually you are developing the internal self-discipline, the internal desire to make good use of your time. This is more important than the desire to do a particular Escape or to avoid a particular A-1. Little by little you are getting more control over your time and over your life.

The better your willpower, the less trouble you'll experience when you want to get involved in a project. You'll have developed the habit of being committed to doing the best you can on *whatever* is in front of you. You'll be a do-it-now person on whatever the A-1 turns out to be.

Although you recognize the limits on your endurance, try to go another sixty seconds before quitting your jogging. Although you can't yet resist seconds on Mom's apple pie, you can ask her to make the second piece a bit smaller than usual. Although you don't like raking the leaves, you realize you're stuck with it and try not to make yourself quite as unhappy as usual. What's the use of complaining to yourself everytime the rake misses a leaf and you have to go back again?

Try to spend a couple of extra minutes on an unpleasant A before calling it a day. Cut back a couple of minutes on the C, even if it's your pet project. Don't turn to the TV for escape from an unpleasant A. Remember: a little more will can eventually build up to a lot more willpower.

23. DO YOUR BEST AND CONSIDER IT A SUCCESS

ARE YOU WILLING TO SPEND every evening this week to make a start on attaining a lifetime goal even though success is not assured? If you don't try, you guarantee failure. If you do try you have the chance to succeed, but failure is still a possibility. What to do?

Most people spend their lives minimizing losses rather than maximizing gains. For example, take reading the Sunday paper. Do you read every page because you're afraid you will miss something? The more you move away from the front page, and those sections that you know interest you, the less news you will find. The result: You waste time reading much that doesn't really interest you, when you could have played with the kids, read a book or worked in your darkroom.

Some people use up valuable time by endlessly weighing pros and cons for fear of taking a wrong step. Making "mistakes" can be a great time-saver. You find out what works by trying. You get rid of unrealistic goals by having tried and failed to accomplish them. For the rest of your life you might have continued to cherish the dream of writing poetry. But now that you've spent several evenings working steadily at it, you can assure yourself that given your personality, poetry is impossible—at least for the present. Forget it and find a more realistic goal instead. What may seem defeating at first is really constructive: You're building bridges that will eventually take you closer to where you really want to be.

Studies have shown that people who hoped (and strived) for success were happier and accomplished more than those who feared (and expected) failure. If you're willing to accept the initial failures on your way to success, you'll find the energy you need to keep digging until you hit pay dirt. Don't be discouraged by "mistakes." Trial and error is part of being human. Think that each "mistake" is bringing you a little closer to eventual success.

I like to call this process "trial and success." I recall a particularly difficult period in my life when things just weren't going well. I kept telling myself that there were only a limited number of "mistakes" possible on my project and that each "mistake" I made brought me closer to what ultimately would work. The important thing was not to make the same "mistake" too often. Sure enough, I finally saw the light—long after I had hoped to be done with my job and after much more effort than I ever imagined at the beginning. From then on, things went better and better. With that experience behind me, I continually look for new areas to make do. It was trial and success.

When you do something you've never done before, no matter how poorly it turns out, you're on your way to doing it better the next time. Whatever happens, you're further along than if you had never done it at all. If it seems hard to accept failure at first, remind yourself of that comforting saying: "If a thing is worth doing, it's worth doing badly!"

The Value of Trial and Success

A dance company was practicing for a new ballet and the leading man held the ballerina incorrectly. The effort looked very ungraceful. The director asked the man whether he wished to repeat the movement. The dancer replied, "No. It's not necessary. Now I know what to do." The failure made the rehearsal a success. The dancer now knew what he had to do. It was trial and success.

In scientific research multiple "failures" commonly lead to success. The combined unsuccessful experiments of Marie Curie, Alexander Fleming, and Louis Pasteur run into the thousands. It would have been easy for any one of them to give up after the first hundred failures or so, but today we might have no radium, no penicillin, and no pasteurized milk.

Or take the following extraordinary personal history of failure:

Lost job, 1832; defeated for legislature, 1832; failed in business, 1833; elected to legislature, 1834; sweetheart died, 1835; had nervous breakdown, 1836; defeated for Speaker, 1838; defeated for nomination for Congress, 1843; elected to Congress, 1846; lost renomination, 1848; rejected for land

officer, 1849; defeated for Senate, 1854; defeated for nomination for Vice-President, 1856; again defeated for Senate,
1858; but in 1860 Abraham Lincoln was elected President of
the United States.

Life can only be led on a "best efforts" basis. To look back
and say "I could have done better" is not realistic. O.K., so
you might have wished to do better. And you can imagine
having done better. But the fact that you *didn't* means that,
under the circumstances, you *couldn't*.

So don't let failure stop you from trying. Don't waste time
worrying about what went "wrong." You can learn something
from every experience. Remember: You're older and wiser
than the last time you dealt with a similar situation, even if it
was only fifteen minutes ago.

The habits of a lifetime cannot be changed in a few days.
It takes time—sometimes a year or two. There is no "Open
Sesame" to getting control of your time and your life. But
you can make much progress toward realizing your everyday
and life goals in even a short time. I encourage you to begin
as soon as you finish this page. I've seen remarkable results
when people apply the techniques I've recommended.

You too can get more enjoyment from every minute, be
more successful in your career and personal life, and accomplish more with less effort. Today can mark a real turning
point for you. You can get more time out of your life.

So what is the best use of your time right now?

APPENDIX

How I Save Time

1. I count all my time as "On-Time" and try to get satisfaction (not necessarily accomplishment) out of every minute.
2. I try to enjoy whatever I am doing.
3. I'm a perennial optimist.
4. I build on successes.
5. I don't waste time regretting my failures.
6. I don't waste my time feeling guilty about what I don't do.
7. I remind myself: "There is always enough time for the important things." If it's important I'll make the time to do it.
8. I try to find a new technique each day that I can use to help gain time.
9. I get up at 5 a.m. during the week (and go to bed early).
10. I have a light lunch so I don't get sleepy in the afternoon.
11. I don't read newspapers or magazines (except occasionally). I do glance at the headlines at the newsstands to keep up on the world.
12. I skim books quickly looking for ideas.
13. I don't own a television set. (My family and I went to a motel to watch the moon walks and we rented a set for the political conventions.)
14. I have my office close enough to my home to be able to walk to work. But when I'm lazy or in a hurry I drive.
15. I examine old habits for possible elimination or streamlining.
16. I've given up forever all "waiting time." If I have to

wait I consider it a "gift of time" to relax, plan or do something I would not otherwise have done.

17. I keep my watch 3 minutes fast, to get a head start on the day.

18. I carry blank 3x5 index cards in my pocket to jot down notes and ideas.

19. I revise my lifetime goals list once a month.

20. I review my lifetime goals list every day and identify activities to do each day to further my goals.

21. I put signs in my office reminding me of my goals.

22. I keep my long-term goals in mind even while doing the smallest task.

23. I always plan first thing in the morning and set priorities for the day.

24. I keep a list of specific items to be done each day, arrange them in priority order, and then do my best to get the important ones done as soon as possible.

25. I schedule my time months in advance in such a way that each month offers variety and balance as well as "open time" reserved for "hot" projects.

26. I give myself time off and special rewards when I've done the important things.

27. I do first things first.

28. I work smarter rather than harder.

29. I try to do only A's, never B's and C's.

30. I have confidence in my judgment of priorities and stick to them in spite of difficulties.

31. I ask myself, "Would anything terrible happen if I didn't do this priority item?" If the answer is no, I don't do it.

32. If I seem to procrastinate I ask myself: "What am I avoiding?"—and then I try to confront that thing head-on.

33. I always use the 80/20 rule.

34. I start with the most profitable parts of large projects and often find it is not necessary to do the rest.

35. I cut off nonproductive activities as quickly as possible.

36. I give myself enough time to concentrate on high priority items.

37. I have developed the ability to concentrate well for long stretches of time (sometimes with the aid of coffee).

38. I concentrate on one thing at a time.

39. I focus my efforts on items that will have the best long-term benefits.
40. I keep pushing and am persistent when I sense I have a winner.
41. I have trained myself to go down my To Do List without skipping over the difficult items.
42. I do much of my thinking on paper.
43. I work alone creatively in the morning and use the afternoons for meetings, if necessary.
44. I set deadlines for myself and others.
45. I try to listen actively in every discussion.
46. I try not to waste other people's time (unless it's something that really matters to me).
47. I delegate everything I possibly can to others.
48. I make use of specialists to help me with special problems.
49. I have someone screen my mail and phone calls and handle all routine matters.
50. I generate as little paperwork as possible and throw away anything I possibly can.
51. I handle each piece of paper only once.
52. I write replies to most letters right on the piece of paper.
53. I keep my desk top cleared for action, and put the most important thing in the center of my desk.
54. I have a place for everything (so I waste as little time as possible looking for things).
55. I save up all trivia for a three-hour session once a month.
56. I try not to think of work on weekends.
57. I relax and "do nothing" rather frequently.
58. I recognize that inevitably some of my time will be spent on activities outside my control and don't fret about it.
59. I keep small talk to a minimum during work hours.
60. I look for action steps to be taken now to further my goals.
61. I'm continually asking myself: "What is the best use of my time right now?"